D1017472

THE
AID
TRAP

R. GLENN HUBBARD / WILLIAM DUGGAN

THE
AID
TRAP

HARD TRUTHS
ABOUT ENDING POVERTY

Columbia Business School
Publishing

COLUMBIA UNIVERSITY PRESS

Publishers Since 1893

New York   Chichester, West Sussex

Copyright © 2009 R. Glenn Hubbard and William Duggan

Library of Congress Cataloging-in-Publication Data

Hubbard, R. Glenn.

The aid trap : hard truths about ending poverty /

R. Glenn Hubbard and William Duggan.

p. cm.

Includes bibliographical references and index.

ISBN 978-0-231-14562-6 (cloth : alk. paper) — ISBN 978-0-231-51950-2 (e-book)

1. Economic assistance—Developing countries.

2. Poverty—Developing countries. 3. Economic development—

Developing countries. I. Duggan, William R. II. Title.

HC60.H8195 2009

338.9109172´4—dc22   2009021579

Columbia University Press books are printed on permanent
and durable acid-free paper.

This book is printed on paper with recycled content.

Printed in the United States of America

c 10 9 8 7 6 5 4 3 2 1

FOR CONSTANCE, RAPH, AND WILL

❁ ❁ ❁

FOR LYNN AND EMMALINE

CONTENTS

PREFACE

THE SOFTWARE OF PROSPERITY

For the third time in a little more than a century, Wall Street is in crisis. The effects have spread throughout the world. The previous crises of 1907 and 1929–32 ended when the American business sector recovered. Around the world today the response so far has been the same: to shore up each country's local business sector. We see a global consensus among prosperous nations that a thriving business sector is the source of their prosperity. They know that their local businesses are the only hope to have enough good-paying jobs for the majority of their people on into the future. These nations are taking massive government action, not to replace the business sector but to revive it.

Not so for many poor countries. Their own governments are mostly anti-business, and the aid that rich countries give them overwhelmingly supports government agencies and nongovernmental organizations (NGOs) rather than business. For some reason, rich countries support business in their own countries but not in poor ones. This book explains the reason and offers an alternative to the current aid system: a large-scale program of pro-business aid for the poor nations of the world.

The leading advocates of the current aid system are celebrities like the rock star Bono, the Columbia economist Jeffrey Sachs, and Bill Gates through his foundation. They argue that rich countries have both the technology that poor countries need to prosper and the wealth to provide it to them. On the other side we have *Africa Unchained* by George Ayittey, *White Man's Burden* by William Easterly, and *Dead Aid* by Dambisa Moyo: They document not only that aid has not made poor countries any more prosperous, but also that the aid system continues to do the same things again and again despite the evidence that they don't work.

Certainly Ayitteh, Easterly, and Moyo are right, that the past forty years of development aid have been a spectacular failure. But that failure was not inevitable, and it does not need to continue. We can go back two decades earlier than that to find one aid program from rich to poor that did work: the Marshall Plan of 1948 to 1951. Postwar America was rich, Europe was poor, and the Marshall Plan helped Europe catch up. Advocates of even more aid through the current system sometimes call for a Marshall Plan today for poor countries. Are they right?

Yes they are, but for reasons that might surprise them. Most of the recent calls for a Marshall Plan for poor countries today mistake what the original Marshall Plan actually did. That mistaken view is that the Marshall Plan gave away food, medicine, and clothing, on one hand, and rebuilt government infrastructure such as ports, railroads, and water systems, on the other. In fact, the Marshall Plan was in the first instance a program not of charity aid or of government infrastructure but of support to local business. It made loans to European companies, who repaid them to their governments, who then spent the funds on ports, railroads, and water supplies. To qualify for the Plan, countries had to enact certain pro-business policies to make sure that their local businesses could use the loans well.

Let's take a page from Bill Gates's own success in the world of business and divide aid into two parts: hardware and software. The hardware is the ports, railroads, and water plants of the Marshall Plan, or the medicines, fertilizers, and boreholes of the current aid system. The software is the loans and funding mechanism of the Marshall Plan, or the government and NGO project mechanism of current aid. The Marshall Plan software works, and the current aid software doesn't. Gates is right that technology is the key to aid, but not the hardware of medicines, fertilizers, and boreholes. Like the source of his own fortune, it's the software that matters most.

This book is about the software of prosperity: the rules, policies, and institutions that govern how business operates in each country and the mechanisms of aid funding that either help or hurt that local business sector. The current world financial crisis is clearly a software problem. That's what everyone's trying to fix for the prosperous countries of the world. World poverty is also a software problem, but the aid system has been trying to fix the hardware instead, and got the software wrong. The Marshall Plan got it right for postwar Europe. For the sake of poor countries, let's hope it's not too late to correct the error and get it right for them too.

❀ ❀ ❀

The authors would like to thank Myles Thompson of Columbia University Press for urging us to write this book, for his precious editorial guidance, and for the chance to contribute to the new imprint of Columbia Business School Publishing. Marina Petrova of the Press worked wonders with the manuscript. And we thank the many students and alumni of Columbia Business School who are ahead of us in both word and deed to help foster a thriving business sector in the poorer countries of the world.

THE
AID
TRAP

1

INTRODUCTION

THE CHARITY TRAP

If you stroll along Wall Street in New York, you see that it ends at Trinity Church. It's a famous view, down the narrow street to the elegant spire of the brownstone church. You can find the view in countless postcards, guides to New York City, and snapshots that tourists took themselves. For two centuries Trinity has been the "Wall Street church," and remains so to this day.

If you went to Trinity on Easter Sunday, 2008, you heard the children's choir and a stirring sermon by the rector. In the Prayers of the People you prayed for the Episcopal Church, the Archbishop of Canterbury, bishops in the United States, and Trinity's companion Diocese of Matlosane, South Africa. You prayed for the American president, the governor of New York State, the mayor of New York City, and the secretary-general of the United Nations. You prayed for the homeless and destitute, for all who have died, and for the Parish mission that proclaims by word and example the Good News of God in Christ.

And you also prayed for this:

> We pray to strengthen our commitment to the Millennium Development Goals, and in support of Counting Prayers, a show of will we say, "The world now has the means to end extreme poverty. We pray that we have the will."

Counting Prayers is a Trinity program that encourages religious congregations of all denominations to support the United Nation's Millennium Development Goals and sponsor Millennium Villages in the poorest countries of the world. One of its aims is a billion prayers for the Goals, and it keeps track online. As of June 11, 2008, the tally was 563,218. When you become a Millennium Congregation, you send money to a Millennium Village, stay in touch with the villagers online, and send your congregation members to visit them. The money goes to help the Village put in place all eight Goals at once:

1. Eradicate extreme poverty and hunger.
2. Achieve universal primary education.
3. Promote gender equality and empower women.
4. Reduce child mortality.
5. Improve maternal health.
6. Combat HIV/AIDS, malaria, and other diseases.

7. Ensure environmental sustainability.
8. Develop a global partnership for development.

Trinity is just one of the many notable supporters of these Millennium Development Goals. Celebrities like the rock star Bono and the Hollywood actress Angelina Jolie are perhaps the most famous examples. The list is long and grows every day. Yet Trinity's support is especially telling on two key counts. First, it shows the roots of the Goals in the timeless and worthy religious desire to help the needy. Second, it takes place literally in the shadow of Wall Street, worldwide home of the real solution to poverty: the business sector.

The Millennium Development Goals are a vehicle for charity. Money from rich countries pays for government agencies and nongovernmental organizations (NGOs) to run projects in poor villages that make people's lives there a little bit better. But such projects have never lifted people out of poverty. We know what does that: the ordinary business sector. Only business creates the jobs that pull people out of poverty. It's the only reliable path to mass prosperity the world has ever known.

Prosperity and poverty are opposites. Poverty is the lack of prosperity, and prosperity is where you arrive when you rise out of poverty. Let's use the most basic definition of prosperity: a decent place to live, decent clothes, food on the table, and enough wealth of some kind—livestock, land, a building, money, jewelry, or other possessions—to survive setbacks like drought, sickness, economic crisis, or war. When large numbers of people achieve that, we can call it "mass" prosperity. The farther back in time we go, the harder it is to estimate how many people were poor or prosperous. Even today we can only make a rough estimate: Of the world's 6.7 billion people, more than 40 percent—almost 3 billion—are poor.

Way back in time, 100 percent of people were poor. With the rise of kings like the pharaohs of Egypt, a tiny percentage—the rulers—were prosperous. The rise of ordinary business then led to mass prosperity for more and more people, to reach today's figure of 60 percent. The ordinary business sector is the best hope for the other 40 percent to rise out of poverty too. Our basic definition of *ordinary business* is this: Private individuals and companies employ people for pay, or people work for themselves as farmers who sell their crops, artisans who sell their wares, merchants who buy and sell what others make, or bankers who finance all of the above. Everywhere business emerged from other systems, so it's often hard to see exactly when business overtook them. For example, in feudal Europe lords started selling crops that their serfs produced. Eventually they were no longer serfs and lords but farmers large and small, and their employees, within a business system.

If you're reading this in a prosperous country, you can see for yourself the simple power of the ordinary business sector. Just take a look around you. What do you see and how did it get there? The furniture in the room you're

in probably came from five or six different furniture businesses that made it, five or six different stores that sold
it, and five or six different shipping companies that got it
from the maker to the store. Same with your clothes. Same
with the food you ate today: A business made it, a store
sold it, and another firm shipped it. Or else you went to a
restaurant—another business. Other businesses sold those
businesses the wood or the cloth or the tomatoes to make
what you use or consume. Behind the scenes, other firms
insured those businesses, gave them loans, or did their
accounting. Some are local and some are based in other
countries. All together they give vital jobs to people in
whatever country they operate in or sell to. Those workers
and the companies themselves pay taxes with the money
they earn, which governments spend on vital services such
as roads and hospitals, or they donate to charities to aid the
poor or help local arts, science, or education.

Go back in time for every region on earth and you will
find that the people there started out poor. You will also
find that there was no business sector. Over the centuries,
at different rates and at different times, ordinary business
grew and spread to more and more parts of the world. Our
most recent examples are India and China: Over the past
two decades they began removing the shackles from their
business sectors, and millions of their citizens rose out of
poverty. There remain millions of poor in India and China,
of course. But business did not make them poor. They were
already poor, going back centuries. The best chance for

these remaining poor to escape poverty is for the business sector in India and China to keep growing, and thriving. The solution to poverty in these formerly destitute countries is not the Millennium Goals, or village NGO projects, but the ordinary growth of a thriving domestic business sector.

Trinity, Bono, Angelina Jolie, and all the contributors to the Millennium Goals have fallen into the charity trap. They themselves owe their prosperity to the business sector, yet for poor countries they offer charity instead. Even Warren Buffet, perhaps the most successful business investor in history (and a graduate of Columbia Business School) falls into the same trap: When he gave $30 billion to the Gates Foundation, he told the press, "The market has not worked in terms of poor people." The truth is, Buffett knows very little about the market in poor countries—he makes his money in rich ones. And Bono, Jolie, and the Trinity parishioners who visit their Villages have hardly studied the economic history of poor countries in any meaningful detail. They just assume that charity is the answer: And that's exactly the trap.

The market has not worked in poor countries because it never had the chance. It's the same story as India and China: In the 1990s their governments finally removed longstanding barriers to ordinary business—especially licensing, where you could not open or invest in any business without an expensive government license, and the government gave out very few of them because of an explicit intention to restrict the business sector. In both countries the results have been dramatic. In the poorest countries of the world, especially Africa, such barriers remain. And in these poorest countries another set of barriers make things even worse: a vast volume of charity aid that crowds out or corrupts the business sector. Since the 1960s, trillions of dollars in charity aid have failed to make a dent in poverty, yet the money continues to flow.

Take the three countries in the world that receive the most aid per local dollar: São Tomé, Guinea-Bissau, and Malawi—all in Africa. The World Bank ranks countries every year on how easy it is for a local citizen to start and run a business: In 2008, these three countries ranked 163rd, 176th, and 127th out of 178 nations on the list. Basically, don't even bother to try. So instead of struggling to start a business, citizens of these countries aspire to work for the government and NGO agencies that deliver the aid. Working as a driver for an aid agency makes you many times more money than working as a farmer or trader. And why should the government of such countries remove the barriers to business when it gets plenty of money from foreign aid? Between government rules and charity money, business hasn't got a prayer.

Think back to the Soviet Union in the 1980s. That's when serious poverty became apparent across the land: Would you have recommended the Millennium Development Goals? Was the answer then an array of village projects funded and run by government agencies and NGOs? Of course not. That's not how to end poverty. Only the business sector can do that. That's what happened in the Soviet Union and its satellites in Eastern Europe after the Berlin wall fell in 1989. Over the past two decades the business sector has grown from nearly nothing in those countries and has gradually brought prosperity to more and more of their people.

But the poorest countries of the world have no single Berlin wall to topple. Hundreds of aid agencies run thousands of aid projects in dozens of countries. Thousands of people who run those agencies—and the millions of good-hearted people who fund them—have all fallen into the same charity trap as Trinity and Bono and Buffett. No single policy change, by one key agency, can reverse the tide. Development charity has become the favorite cause of schoolchildren in rich countries, high school seniors feature it on their college applications, and the list of celebrities who add their names and millions is growing all the time. Charity aid is here to stay, no matter what damage some of it causes.

Yet all is not lost. We cannot and should not stop the flow of aid. There will always be a role for charity, as there still is in all rich countries. Giving food, clothing, shelter, and medicine to the poor is a long and noble tradition. It is a biblical certainty that the poor will always be with us, and charity helps keep them alive. That is a very good thing. But it's very different from aid for economic development, to bring people out of poverty. For that we must direct aid to support the business sector. And we have a stellar model: the Marshall Plan of post–World War II Europe. Many people think that the Marshall Plan was charity aid: food, clothing, and medicine for war-torn Europe. But that was the United Nations Relief and Rehabilitation Administration, which wrapped up its work in 1947. The Marshall Plan came later. Its single aim was a thriving domestic business sector in every single country. And it worked. Aid can indeed help to end poverty, by helping the business sector. The Marshall Plan shows how.

This book makes the case for why and how to divert a major share of aid from charity to business in poor countries. In the first half of the book we study the history of prosperity around the world—how all countries started out poor but some, over time, rose out of poverty. In all cases, business played the key role. Next we move to countries that have not escaped from poverty, where we see how anti-business policies and practices have kept prosperity at bay. And we find out in detail how the aid system of the past forty years—of which the Millennium Development Goals are just the latest round—makes it even harder for business to thrive in the countries that need it most.

In the second half of the book we learn how the Marshall Plan worked and how to adapt it to poor countries today. Europe after World War II is very different from the poor countries of the twenty-first century, so the Marshall mechanisms need prudent adaptation to the present day. We work through the details of the program, organization and funding for a Marshall-type aid system at a large enough scale to make a big enough difference in as many poor countries as decide to join in. And from that we discover what everyone can do to help: how to take the same energy, good will, time, and money that so many organizations and individuals devote to charity aid and apply some of it to helping business instead.

Business will never touch the heart the way charity does. Some of those Trinity parishioners want to pay for a well in a village and then go visit to see it working. There is nothing wrong with that desire, but typically they remain completely unaware of the damage behind the scenes: how a local well-digging company can never compete with a foreign charity that digs wells for free. But there are ways to help the well company too, and that's the path out of poverty. Charity and business are equally worthy, equally possible to support with aid, and equally vital to saving the world.

2

BUSINESS FIRST

The Roots of Prosperity in the Modern World

I n this chapter we trace the history of economic success around the globe, from the dawn of history to the present day. We note especially the role of business in helping countries make the shift from mass poverty to mass prosperity over the centuries. We see that no two countries ever follow identical paths or end up in exactly the same place. But there is a clear pattern: Large numbers of people rise out of poverty as elements of a thriving business sector replace the previous economic system. In all cases it was a struggle: Some form of competing system resisted the change. And in the case of countries that have remained poor, that competing system is still winning.

Let's begin with an inventory of what makes up a thriving business sector. We'll use the same annual World Bank report that ranks countries every year, the *Doing Business* series. Here are the elements it tracks:

1. Starting a business.
2. Dealing with licenses.
3. Employing workers.
4. Registering property.
5. Getting credit.
6. Protecting investors.
7. Paying taxes.
8. Trading across borders.
9. Enforcing contracts.
10. Closing a business.

Overall, prosperous countries rank high on the list, and poor countries rank low. For example, in 2008 Singapore ranked first out of 178 countries, and Congo-Kinshasa ranked last. In this chapter we ask: How did this gap between pro-business and anti-business countries happen? And if the benefits of business are so clear, why hasn't every country jumped on the wagon? The answers to these questions give us key insights into the struggles of business in poor countries today.

We start at the dawn of history: when writing first appeared. We know something of prehistory through archeology, oral traditions, and the study of language and DNA traits across the world. But writing is key to the history of prosperity, because record keeping is a universal key to a thriving business sector. Humans likely traded with each other since the dawn of time, but keeping records helps you plan and keep track of a much larger volume of business than just your memory alone.

Scholars judge that the earliest writing appeared around 5000 B.C. in three irrigated river valleys: Egypt, Upper India, and Mesopotamia, in what is now Iraq. Mesopotamia was the first to develop a full system of writing, by around 3000 B.C. The oldest examples we have are carved tablets of clay and stone. They seem to be records of grain and other goods that kings collected from their subjects as tax and then parceled back out to them as stipends. Archeologists have found money and goods in various sites from the same era that tell us the towns of Mesopotamia were already centers of local and long-distance trade and makers of pottery and other simple products for sale. After 2500 B.C. we find the first records of loans between individuals, as advances to ordinary citizens to pay taxes and as finance to merchants for trade.

These ancient loan contracts are the oldest written evidence of private business on earth. They start our list of ten business elements with number 5: "Getting credit." We know there was a high volume of loans, because kings sometimes issued decrees that abolished the debts of ordinary citizens, who sometimes sold themselves into temporary slavery to pay back their advances. The decrees did not affect loans between merchants. By 2000 B.C., loan contracts were the most common written document among all Mesopotamian records. The king set the interest rate: For centuries it stood at one fifth for silver and one third for grain, per year. The famous Code of Hammurabi—the first written laws in history, around 1750 B.C.—gives this same formula. In practice, contracts often added or subtracted from the official rate.

Which came first, commercial loans or a business sector? It's a chicken-and-egg problem for scholars. The answer seems to be that the two arose together. In archeological sites older than 2500 B.C. throughout the world, you sometimes find pottery or tools from far away. That means some form of trade existed among people as far back in time as we can reach. But that is different from a specialized group of people who handle the trade: merchants who buy and sell, bankers who lend them money, and transporters by caravan or boat. Add to them the artisans who use the goods flowing through to make and sell crafts: for example, a potter who uses the clay right there instead of sending it through to its original destination. It's most efficient if these specialists are close together in one commercial center, because they all do business with each other. And they all need loans, which are also easier to collect and repay when the borrower and lender are nearby.

From Mesopotamia, loans with interest spread throughout the Middle East and into the Mediterranean. The Phoenicians, Greeks, Persians, and Romans adopted them in turn. Thousands of trading cities and towns across these empires sprang up as local centers of commerce. In these ancient sites we see the first glimmers of mass prosperity as we defined it in the last chapter: large numbers of people with enough income and wealth for a decent life. Archeologists uncovered in large numbers of dwellings an abundance of pottery, metal implements, mosaics and sculptures, and many workshops for the many craft shops that sold their goods near and far. The archeologists found few of these items in the countryside, where most people lived. Scholars cite such possessions as evidence of mass prosperity. As a percentage of the world's total population, these commercial centers were always a small fraction. But within these towns, for the first time in history large numbers of ordinary people were no longer poor. They give us the first glimpse of greater prosperity to come, as that same business system spread over the centuries to more and more people throughout the world.

What kept this ancient business sector so small? First of all, we must keep in mind the overall poverty of the world at that time. Almost everyone farmed, almost wholly for themselves, with simple implements and methods that kept their yields low. They handed over some of their crops as tax to their ruler. From earliest times there was a lively trade in grain and other food, but it remained a tiny percentage of the total harvest. The most prosperous farms were close to the commercial centers and tied to them through agricultural loans and merchants buying and selling land. For most of the world beyond the commercial centers, life was hard and short. There was no money for schools, and children worked hard from an early age, so literacy remained very low. Disease took a heavy toll.

Second, war and pillage destroyed commerce again and again over the centuries. Armed men arrived to steal everything of value, kill and rape, and often destroy the town itself. This produced temporary prosperity among the mass of soldiers. But once the loot ran out, they had to raid again. Or they too were raided and lost everything. Mass prosperity endured only as long as an empire's army succeeded in protecting its business sector from other empires, and more important, from thousands of smaller tribes and kingdoms surrounding them that kept on raiding the towns.

It was not until the first two centuries A.D. that one empire—Rome—managed to preserve peace long enough for prosperity to spread beyond its ancient limits to more people, through the rapid rise and growth of thousands of commercial centers with their nearby farmlands. But even then life expectancy was only twenty-five years. And in the third and fourth centuries A.D., war disrupted Roman business again. In the fifth century the Roman Empire fell.

Let's look at the Roman Empire in those two peaceful centuries, to take stock of our ten elements from *Doing Business*. The first one, *Starting a business*, seemed easy enough. There was no particular restriction or even procedure for anyone to open a business, including women, non-Romans, and slaves. In practice, of course, other aspects of Roman society made it far easier for Roman men to open a business than anyone else: They took all the good government posts, especially in the army, which gave them income to start a business. And most businesses had to do business with other businesses to some degree, and in that

Roman men favored each other. We see the same thing in many countries today, where the rules say anyone can own a business but various forms of social discrimination keep out women or certain ethnic groups. From Rome to the present day, it's always best to open business to everyone, both in law and in fact.

The second element, *Dealing with licenses*, also seemed easy, with the same caveats as those for *Starting a business*, with one big exception. Anyone could make, buy, or sell anything, without any license at all, except for government monopolies. The Empire ran its own mines for salt, metal, and marble. It bought or taxed grain directly from farmers and distributed it to citizens in the cities. And it produced all its own uniforms, weapons, and other supplies for its army. The government did buy some of its supplies from private businesses, and sometimes turned a blind eye—or a corrupt one—to private trade in these items. So business needed no government licenses, but a vast volume of business remained in government rather than private hands.

The third element, *Employing workers*, was much too easy for a healthy business sector. Instead of paying wages, an employer could buy a slave. As it fought and conquered, the Roman army sent a steady stream of slaves to the mines, farms, and towns. In town, some became household servants, but most worked in some kind of private business. The town slaves were the lucky ones. Slavery was an ancient evil that long predated the Roman business system. As Roman business grew, it depended more on ordinary hiring and less on slaves. There seemed to be no restriction against businesses hiring and firing ordinary wage workers, or against workers taking jobs and quitting them. We can even recognize a modern business manager in the Roman *institore*, who ran an enterprise for the absentee owner.

The fourth element, *Registering property*, was also much too easy for a healthy business sector, for the same reason: slavery. Thanks to Rome's advanced legal system, written laws allowed and protected individuals to own and sell property of all kinds. On the one hand, that's good for business. On the other hand, property included slaves. But again outside the evils of slavery, for registering other property the Roman system was good.

The fifth element, *Getting credit*, saw Rome inherit the ancient loan system of Mesopotamia. The Roman legal system allowed and protected loans with interest as a form of contract. Banks began to develop, as some merchants specialized in money-lending and took deposits that paid interest. But the volume of loans stayed small. The old Roman ruling class was made up of feudal lords and government officials who looked down on business as a lowly occupation. Their wealth came from land, olive groves, cattle, slaves, and taxes. So few of the wealthy invested their riches in banks. With no big banks to borrow from, the government paid for a larger army by raising taxes. When centuries of peace gave way to centuries of war, the larger and larger army called for more and more taxes. That crippled the business sector. It was one of the reasons Rome finally fell.

The sixth element, *Protecting investors*, got a small start before the Empire ended. There were no real corporations, where individuals pooled money for a single ongoing enterprise. The category did not even exist in Roman law. Without corporations there are no investors to protect. But there was one kind of business that came close: a "society" that took long-term contracts to collect taxes for the government. This made for a predictable, stable investment. Romans bought and sold shares in the societies, and Roman law protected these sales as ordinary contracts. If society managers embezzled money, you could take them to court and win. For this one early form of semi-corporation, Rome did protect investors.

The seventh element, *Paying taxes*, was no special burden for business, except during wars. There was no special business tax. A business owner paid one annual tax of 1 to 3 percent on property and wealth, just like everyone else. For comparison: In the Congo Republic today, *Doing Business* reports that a company makes eighty-nine payments over the year, using up 106 workdays for paperwork and waiting in line, to pay taxes that take 65.4 percent of its profits.

The eighth element, *Trading across borders*, benefited from the Empire's great size. From Britain to Syria there were no borders, so no customs duties to pay. Even crossing into the Empire, merchants paid duties of only around 5 percent, which is very low by any standard, ancient or modern. And paying the duty took a few hours at most. *Doing Business* tells us that within sub-Saharan Africa today it takes an average of thirty-five days to export goods across a border, thanks to all the paperwork and fees to pay.

The ninth element, *Enforcing contracts*, was the pride of the Roman legal system. Courts throughout the Empire made contracts easy to create and easy to enforce. The contract was either written or oral with witnesses who could later testify in court. But were the courts fair? Could you bribe a judge, or did the judge obey the government rather than the law? Corruption was certainly an ongoing problem in the Roman Empire. But the government clearly made certain that business could thrive in those two centuries of peace. At least in that period the courts aided rather than preyed on the ordinary flow of daily business.

The tenth element, *Closing a business,* is mostly about bankruptcy: How much does it cost, in time and money, to end your business, and can your creditors get some of their money back? Because there was no special category of corporation, Roman law treated bankruptcy as unpaid debts under contract law. The court let you seize the property of others or force them to be your slave if they failed to pay. And in a "society" of several individuals, if one of them incurred huge personal debts outside the business, the court would seize not only the business but the personal property of all the other members. These rules worked against business, as they did not allow entrepreneurs to recover from failure and try again.

All in all, *Doing Business* would give the Roman Empire in the first two centuries A.D. a fairly high score on most of its indicators. Slavery, the absence of true corporations, and the seizure of property were the biggest drawbacks. The greatest strengths were a legal and government system that helped ordinary business spread easily throughout the Empire. And spread it did: pottery and glass makers, grain and wine merchants, tailors, butchers, carpentry and metal workshops, bakers, oil presses, linen and wool weavers, sellers of hides and fish, lamp makers, jewelers, ivory and ebony traders, and dozens of other types of business sprang up in the thousands of trading cities and towns that thrived wherever the Roman army kept the peace. The greatest volume of trade was within and between the Roman provinces, back and forth across the expanding Empire. The government-built roads and ports were needed, first for its conquering army and then for the commerce that followed.

After 500 A.D., as the vast Roman Empire fell to wave after wave of tribal armies, its business towns died out. But over the next few centuries, three successors arose in the former Roman lands: the Byzantine Empire of the northeast, the Arab Caliphate of the east and south, and the Holy Roman Empire in the west. Ruling from in what is today Istanbul, the Byzantines preserved some of the Roman business system, but tended more to the practices of the older empires like those of Egypt and China. Rulers were despots who squeezed wealth out of their subjects through high taxes, outright seizure, and government monopoly of trade. Ruling from Baghdad, the Arabs at first adopted and then improved upon the Roman business system. The founder of the Caliphate, Mohammed, was a trader himself. Arab mathematicians invented algebra, which allowed merchants to calculate multi-year interest. Widespread religious instruction and courts on the Jewish model helped spread basic accounting skills and resolved myriad business disputes.

For a time the Byzantine and Arab empires thrived. But there was hardly peace: The two empires constantly fought each other and then the Holy Roman Empire on their western frontiers. In the midst of war, the business sectors of the two eastern empires had little chance to develop beyond their Roman roots. War strengthened the despotic tendencies in both empires. Then they fell to other despots: The Mongols took the Caliphate in 1258, then the Ottomans defeated the Byzantines in 1453 and took over the Caliphate in 1535.

The Holy Roman Empire took a very different path. The tribal invasions that defeated Rome broke up the European countryside into hundreds of separate kingdoms. Charlemagne of the Franks was the first to reassemble a sizable empire and crowned himself Holy Roman Emperor in 800 A.D. Charlemagne's feudal system became the model for the rest of Europe except where the Byzantines, Arabs, or Ottomans ruled, such as Greece, Spain, and Hungary.

The Holy Roman Empire was a new kind of system: feudal rather than despotic. Despotic emperors enforced absolute rule through a central army funded with taxes and plunder both internal and external. In feudalism the central army in large part came instead from the armies of each subject kingdom, whose armies in turn came from their subject regions, whose armies in turn came from their local lords, who called up their serfs to arms. Charlemagne spread the system through direct conquest. His enemies adopted it too, as protection from him, from the tribes that beat Rome, from each other, and from Byzantine, Arab, and Ottoman armies.

This pyramid structure of Charlemagne proved flexible and strong, as kingdoms, regions, and lords switched allegiances as armies won and lost on the battlefield. For the next ten centuries, from 800 to 1800 A.D., feudal kingdoms and empires rose and fell and fought with each across western Europe. Business suffered greatly, for two reasons. First, yet again the constant warfare was bad for business. Second, the Charlemagne model was strongly anti-business. Instead of business transactions, goods and money flowed up through the pyramid as taxes from a peasant's field, to a lord, to a prince, to the king. At every level the Catholic Church oversaw the flow, took a cut, and enforced policies that helped suppress business outside this system. That's what made the empire "Holy."

The most important anti-business policy of the feudal empires of western Europe was a religious ban on giving loans with interest. This effectively banned all Catholics from the business sector, which greatly reduced its overall size and crippled it to the core. In eastern Europe some

Greeks and Syrians ranged out from the Byzantine Empire to trade with the west—as Orthodox Christians rather than Catholics, they were exempt from the ban. But in most of western Europe, out of reach of Byzantium, Jews became the merchants. Their system of teaching their children to read and write had given Jews an advantage across the Roman Empire, and they carried that tradition into the heart of Europe. They kept up their trading contacts with fellow Jews in the Arab and Byzantine empires too. Centuries after the fall of Rome, Jews kept business alive in Europe.

In some ways, the anti-business system of feudal Europe had much in common with despotic empires that developed strong bureaucracies. Egyptian pharaohs and the emperors of ancient and classical China and Egypt supplemented military rule with paid officials who kept tight control over economic life. The Ottomans began as military despots and over time developed a despotic bureaucracy too, based on Arab and Byzantine literate traditions. In the Holy Roman Empire the feudal warlords who ruled western Europe lacked the tradition of literacy that bureaucracy needed. That vanished with the fall of Rome. The Catholic Church stepped into the breach, with its vast system of religious training in a common language across Europe: Latin, inherited from the Romans. Each feudal lord had a corresponding Church official, in principle loyal both to him and the pope, to run the legal system in his domain.

Despotic bureaucracies differed from feudal bureaucracies in how much the ruler depended on a rural elite for power. This is a technical difference, not a moral one: Feudal rule can be just as cruel as despotic rule. Common to feudal and despotic bureaucracies was the suppression of business beyond the control of the ruler. In a bureaucracy, rulers can pick and choose who benefits from the system and dismiss anyone they judge disloyal. In contrast, a thriving business sector allows people to rise in wealth and power that the rulers do not choose. The newly risen might try to turn the tables and pick their own rulers instead. In its early days the Holy Roman Empire fought for survival against tribal kingdoms and powerful rivals, so we can understand the value of such a tight system of political control. But in suppressing the business sector, the feudal system failed to spread prosperity beyond the small ruling circle.

Among the despotic bureaucracies, Egypt endured mostly unchanged for thirty centuries, until it fell to the Greeks and then the Romans. The Ottomans lasted until their defeat in World War I. China became more pro-business under the Tang Dynasty, starting in the seventh century A.D., as the Silk Road to the Arab, Byzantine, and European empires brought business to its doorstep. But the Tang fell to another dynasty in 907, and the bureaucracy took over again. China's vast and fertile farmlands created a prosperous class of landlords, but they joined with the bureaucracy to suppress a business system. As Angus Maddison tells us in *Chinese Economic Performance in the Long Run*:

The bureaucracy and gentry ... prevented the emergence of an independent commercial and industrial bourgeoisie on the European pattern. Entrepreneurial activity was insecure in a framework where legal protection for private activity was so exiguous. Any activity that promised to be lucrative was subject to bureaucratic squeeze. Larger undertakings were limited to the state or to publicly licensed monopolies. Potentially profitable activity in opening up world trade by exploiting China's sophisticated shipbuilding and navigational knowledge was simply forbidden.

It was a similar story in India. Business did better in Southeast Asia, where fertile river valleys on the mainland and the good volcanic soils of Indonesia combined with good ports and trade routes, beyond the direct control of the Chinese and Indian empires. Yet when kingdoms grew in these regions, they took those same empires as models, including their anti-business policies.

Europe's feudal bureaucracy tried just as hard as China's and India's to suppress the business sector. But they failed. So that was where the business sector took off, centuries after Rome fell. Because of its many mountains and valleys, its long and jagged coastline, Europe for over a thousand years remained immune to conquest by any one if its empires or a foreign invader. Instead of a single bureaucracy, uniform and powerful, a jumble of competing kingdoms rose and fell, with never the same borders twice.

In this disorder a new commercial system arose, first to equal and then to surpass its Roman heritage. It started in Venice, just beyond the borders of the Arab Empire to the south, the Byzantine Empire to the east, and the Holy Roman Empire to the north. Venice traded with and between all three. From Venice the new system spread to Genoa and other northern Italian cities, and then across Europe, and finally across the world.

Venice essentially reconstructed the Roman business system and improved on the Roman corporation. Early Venice had the "fraternity," where brothers kept their family business together after the death of the father. In the 1100s this evolved into a "company," where non-family could join in too. The company was a contract to undertake specific activities for a specific time, usually the trading voyage by a single ship, with a specific return for each member. You then renewed it for the next voyage, changing as needed the list of contributors, their contributions, and their return. The partners kept decision-making control, while outsiders just put in money. That outsider contribution was essentially an interest-bearing deposit, much like a modern bond.

But like the Roman "society," the Venetian company still came with unlimited liability for all the partners. A huge personal debt by one could ruin them all. Limiting the contract to a single voyage kept the risk down, because you could eject a reckless partner at that point. But that prevented companies from growing in scale and expanding operations to more than one line of business. And those reckless partners did a good job of hiding their debts until it was too late. Often companies did collapse, in Venice, but the volume of business meant that no single collapse by any one company could disrupt the whole economy. For every one that failed, dozens of others still thrived.

The key to the new Venetian system was not that the "company" was so different from the Roman "society," but that companies dominated the economy completely. The Roman Empire was overall a despotic system with some feudalism in Italy itself and a business sector that grew larger in peace and shriveled in war. Venice, in contrast, was all business. It was a nation of companies, completely outside the European feudal system. It began as a trading town on marshy islands safe from pirates and hostile navies. The business owners elected a Great Assembly, a Senate, and a doge as chief official. There was no hereditary king, no role for the Church, and no ban on Christians charging interest. Pawnbrokers, deposit banks, and merchant banks gave loans large and small to individuals and companies. Low taxes on a large volume of trade paid for a strong army and navy to protect the system from marauding pirates, tribes, kingdoms, and empires.

As the Venetian system spread up the fertile Po Valley and across northern Italy, it began to look like the modern business sector we know today. Large numbers of ordinary people prospered as never before. From Venice in the east to Turin in the west, and in the countryside all along, everyone had a part in the business system. The cities and towns were centers of craft and commerce, and in the countryside between, feudal lords and independent farmers sold them crops, livestock, and land. Those lords began to invest in banks and factories in the towns. By the end of the fifteenth century the Venetian business system dominated all of northern Italy. For the first time in history, business centers and their surrounding farmland were no longer islands of prosperity in the sea of larger despotic empires. In northern Italy the business system was now the sea.

Three features of the Venetian system were still thoroughly unmodern, though: slavery, the exclusion of women from business life, and religious discrimination. You might still have to work off your debts as a slave, and Venetian merchants bought and sold slaves in open markets wherever they roamed. As for the exclusion of women, it would be many centuries before the business sector in Europe and then other countries made much progress there. And Jewish and Muslim merchants in Venice were second-class citizens in matters other than commerce. But for daily business, Venice was more hospitable to Jews and Muslims than anywhere else in Europe.

The new merchants of northern Italy traded east along the Silk Road as far as China. Marco Polo was one of them. In the west they reached Greenland and around Europe to the North Sea. Everywhere they spread the seeds of their business practices. Northern Italy finally fell to the feudal empires of Spain and France around 1500, but the seeds of the

Venetian system had already spread. They fell on the most fertile ground in northern Europe. There the old Roman cities and towns came back to life, as business slowly revived and struggled to free itself from the feudal system.

The most important northern cities that had been Roman towns included Strasbourg on the French-German border, Bern in Switzerland, Lyon in France, and London and Manchester in England. Thousands of smaller old Roman towns revived as well. Beyond the old Roman territories the Venetian system spread east to newer towns and cities along the coast and inland from the North and Baltic seas, with Lübeck and Hamburg as the main centers on either side of the Danish peninsula. These coastal towns and their hinterlands formed the Hanseatic League. By the late fourteenth century it rivaled northern Italy in its thorough adoption of the business system.

In town after town, committees of traders across northern Europe wrested from their feudal rulers the same kind of self-government that Venice pioneered. Business owners elected their own representatives to run the towns alone or jointly with the local feudal ruler. The local lord always tried to stop them by force of arms, but over time, in town after town, the lords gave in. One key advantage was that the feudal lords competed with each other, in both war and lavish lifestyle, and so relied on the town merchants for taxes and frequent loans. Yet even when the town gained independence from the local lord, it pledged allegiance and paid taxes higher up, to the king.

For example, the Hanseatic cities owed allegiance directly to the Holy Roman emperor. The feudal rulers of northern Europe let the towns grow, but never enough to overthrow the feudal system.

Except, of course, for Holland. The Dutch fought for and won their independence from feudal Spain in 1581. They elected local rulers and a national stadtholder, much like Venice's doge. Amsterdam became the Venice of the north. Like the Italians, the Dutch traded by ship all over the world. But they had two extra advantages: Northern Europe was far more fertile than southern Europe, and the Dutch sat at the mouth of the Rhine River. More and more farmers across northern Europe produced for sale and so invested in plows and horses to pull them, and the extra food allowed many more hands to turn to crafts for sale, such as woolen cloth. Europe overall has many rivers long and flat enough for boats to carry goods back and forth from the hinterland to the sea, and that sped trade and the growth of towns all along their banks.

The Rhine became the greatest European trading river, because it led from a vast fertile hinterland to a major free trading city on the sea: Amsterdam. That was similar to the Po Valley and Venice, but the Rhine hinterland was far larger. And the lands right around Venice were less fertile than farther upriver, while the richest farmland of the Rhine Valley was at its mouth in Holland. Time and place conspired to make Holland in the 1600s the first country in history where prosperity spread to almost everyone.

All of Holland threw itself into some kind of business. In northern Italy and the Hanseatic League the business system touched everyone and dominated town and country, but alongside a weakened feudalism that kept trying to extract more taxes and prevented its serfs especially from entering fully into business. As a serf you might sell some vegetables or livestock at the market, but you still owed most of your land, labor, and crop to your lord. In Holland that system died out. There were no more lords. The business system replaced the feudal system completely.

In the countryside the Dutch grew crops for sale. In the towns they worked in crafts or commerce, especially financing and shipping goods up and down the Rhine and everywhere Dutch ships sailed. For example, the farmers around the town of Oudewater specialized in growing hemp, and the town made it into rope. Each sailing ship needed about 10 miles of rope. The town workshops also used the hemp to make clothes, paint, oil, and soap. The hemp business alone employed thousands of Dutch farmers and workers. Leiden specialized in wool cloth, which employed even more workers than hemp. Delft made fine pottery. The countryside around Gouda and Edam made cheeses, and the towns sold it. The financing, transport, local sale, and export of these products made even more jobs. Add to those the imports from overseas trade, such as spices, tea, coffee, and Asian cotton. With no competing system everyone in Holland worked in business, and everyone rose out of poverty.

Jews especially moved to Amsterdam and brought the Venice model with them. There they helped the Dutch make further improvements. In 1602, the Dutch East India Company thus became the world's first company financed completely by public shares. The Venetian "company" was still a partnership, where the members had full liability for each other's personal debts, while the outside bondholders just contributed funds in exchange for interest. The East India Company essentially converted those bondholders into stockholders for the whole company. And the Venetian company contract lasted only as long as a single voyage. You could renew it, but only for the same voyage on the same ship. Dutch merchants converted that into an ongoing contract where anyone could withdraw at any time and get their money back.

That was how the East India Company started, but seven years later it declared its shares non-refundable. It would no longer give you your money back. If you wanted out, you had to sell your shares to someone else. And so was born, in 1609, the first truly modern corporation. Buying and selling those shares made Amsterdam the first true stock exchange in the world.

The whole point of this new form was speed and scale: Now that Portuguese explorers had found a sea route east around Africa, the Dutch wanted a way to launch quickly an armada of trading ships to take advantage of the new sea trade with Asia. It worked. From 1610 to 1650, the company paid an average annual dividend of 16.5 percent. The value of the shares created an immediate market in futures and options. The Dutch courts recognized and protected all these variations on financial contracts. More companies issued stock on the Amsterdam exchange, and prospered too.

The Dutch system spread slowly to other cities and countries of Europe, and quickly to England. Among the feudal lands of Europe, the island of Britain was a special case. Feudalism came to England with the French Norman conquest of 1066. For centuries after that the island was safe from invasion. That made England's feudal rulers less fearful that independent merchants would shift allegiance to a competing king. On the European continent ongoing competition among the French, Spanish, and Holy Roman empires kept feudalism more severe than in England. Fewer wars among competing rulers meant that English lords did not have to squeeze their merchants dry to pay for them. They could tax them instead, at a level that kept them in business. And the English hinterland was as fertile as the rest of northern Europe: London grew up at the mouth of the Thames, in the same way that Venice grew up at the mouth of the Po and Amsterdam at the mouth of the Rhine.

In that way London became a smaller version of Amsterdam. In 1600, its merchants founded the English East India Company with many of the same features as the Dutch version, except that the stock was held jointly in private hands rather than by public sale open to anyone. But the English stock exchange took another century to arise, because

England's feudal system fought back far more fiercely than Holland's. In the 1640s the new business class finally overthrew the king, to start a decade of civil war. As in most of Europe, the struggle took on a religious cast: the old Catholic feudal system versus the new Protestant business system. England's isolation gave it a twist: Most Catholics there were not Roman Catholics but Anglo-Catholics, with the king as head of the church. In the end the Protestants invited in a Dutch army of 20,000, who marched to London and put on the throne the Dutch stadtholder, William of Orange.

That was 1688. England quickly adopted the full range of Dutch business practices. The London stock exchange opened in 1698. England lagged Holland in religious tolerance, though: Jews were now free to live and do business there, but religious discrimination against them, and against Roman Catholics, endured. And the English king ended up back on the throne, yielding power gradually, decade by decade, to the rising business class.

The Anglo-Dutch system spread most quickly to their new colonies of America— especially New York, founded by the Dutch in 1624 and taken by the English in 1674. Once again, Jews played a key role in this new business city. Some English settlers tried to construct the old feudal system in America, but overall these new colonies were creatures of the advanced Anglo-Dutch business system. Sure enough, England's American colonies eventually fought and won their independence from the English king. Their victory in

1781 helped inspire the French Revolution eight years later, and then Napoleon's campaigns beyond France.

The 1800s saw the other kings of Europe fall one by one, first to Napoleon and then to internal events. Historians refer to that century as the "bourgeois revolution," where the business class—the bourgeoisie—replaced feudal aristocrats across Europe. A key year was 1848, when dozens of uprisings across Europe aimed to depose local kings or made them share power with the new business class. In France, for example, the king returned to the throne after Napoleon fell, but the 1848 uprising forced him to step down again, never to return to power. Elsewhere most of the uprisings failed in the short term, but over the following decades the business class won more and more concessions from their feudal rulers. By 1900, kings still ruled most of Europe, but business employed most of the people. The big exceptions were Russia, Spain, and Portugal, where the old feudal system stayed strong and business lagged.

In the nineteenth century the Anglo-Dutch system became Euro-American, because that was how far it spread. From Europe and the United States it spread throughout the world. The old Spanish and Portuguese colonies spread feudalism, but the newer colonies of England, Holland, France, and Germany promoted business. Instead of adding colonies the United States expanded its territory from the Atlantic to the Pacific and imposed its business system directly. The spread of business to Asia, Africa, Central and South America brought islands of prosperity to them, much as Roman commercial centers sprang up in the far-off lands that Rome conquered. The benefits of course went first of all to the foreigners, as Romans kept the best business for themselves in their provinces—at first. Over the decades and then centuries, the provincial peoples learned the Roman system and worked their way up to prosperity within it. The same began to happen in the European colonies, on into the twentieth century.

On the other hand, there were plenty of cases where European commerce overseas brought misery, not prosperity, on into the nineteenth century. In North and South America, Old World diseases wiped out most of the native Indians. Then colonists killed the rest or took almost all their land. At the same time, Spanish and Portuguese and then English and Dutch traders bought slaves in Africa and sold them to European colonies and then the United States. In Asia, British gunboats forced opium grown in India onto the Chinese market. And where European colonists came to stay, discrimination against native peoples and the descendants of former slaves continues to this day.

Such evils in the new colonies, unfortunately, have many parallels in the Old World too. Human cruelty is nothing new. Roman armies slaughtered whole tribes. So did Charlemagne. In 1258 the Mongols slaughtered the entire population of Baghdad, capital of the Arab Empire. In Europe Christians killed Jews and Protestants, and Catholics killed each other. Chiefs across West Africa captured slaves and brought them to the coast for European traders to buy.

The business system arose from and coexisted for centuries with barbaric systems that held life cheap. In its early days, business culture was no more or less barbaric than whatever culture it found around it. Over time, as it spread to more of the world and matured for centuries in early havens like Holland, business developed its own specific culture that stood apart from its surroundings.

In nineteenth-century Europe this culture carried the name "liberal." The liberals were the business class. The "conservatives" were the feudal class. Overall, the liberals won. But in the struggle, a new competitor arose: the socialist system. At first it was only an idea, put forth most famously by Karl Marx and Friedrich Engels in their *Communist Manifesto* of 1848—the same year as the bourgeois rebellions against conservative governments across Europe. Just as business seemed to gain the upper hand against its old enemy, a new enemy appeared on the scene. In his *Manifesto* and then his great work *Das Kapital* of 1867, Marx championed a third class, opposed to both the business liberals and the feudal conservatives: the socialist workers. Over the next century Marx's socialist ideas and then the socialist system spread to embrace nearly half the world.

In its most basic form, Marx's core idea has a timeless anti-business appeal. In ancient Mesopotamia, the king periodically wiped away the loans that ordinary people owed to merchants. Christianity and Islam made charging interest a sin against God, although first the Arabs and then the Christians found a way around that, both with the help of Jews exempt from the religious ban. Despite the prosperity that business brought as it spread, its uneven rewards through space and time kept anti-business sentiment alive. Farmers sold their grain to the mill and saw the miller grow richer than them. Or the trader brought in cheaper grain from elsewhere and the local farmers got less for theirs. When the trader was Jewish, anti-business sentiment blended with anti-Semitism to make the problem worse.

Marx's great achievement was to turn this ancient resentment into a system of action. He explained that all profit was a form of theft: The miller gave the farmer less than the grain was worth, as the factory owner paid the worker less than the finished product sold for. That profit was really the property of the farmer and worker. The socialist system was Marx's way for the farmer and worker to get that profit back. In its pure Marxist form socialism eliminates the business sector completely: Farmers and workers take over the state, which then seizes and runs all the mills and factories and divides the profit among the farmers and workers. Problem solved.

In most of Europe pure socialism never won out. A milder form of socialism kept business in private hands but made a variety of concessions to workers, such as weekends off, sick pay, or unemployment insurance. All prosperous countries today boast some form of milder socialism of this kind. Meanwhile, Marx's pure socialism made its biggest converts where business and liberalism lagged.

The Russian tsars managed to fend off European liberalism, so by 1900, Russia was the most feudal state in Europe. In 1905, an uprising led to a liberal government that shared power with the tsar, but both the liberals and the tsar proved no match for the Red Army of 1918. Russia became a pure socialist state.

As liberalism spread to eastern Asia, feudal Japan embraced it wholesale in 1868, while feudal China took smaller steps. In 1911, a liberal government replaced the Chinese emperor but found itself no match for the warlords who exploited a weak central government throughout China's history. One warlord, General Chiang Kai-Shek, rose above the others but proved no match for the Red Army of the late 1940s. China became a pure socialist state. By internal rebellion and the aid, threat, or use of Russian or Chinese military might, the pure socialist system spread from those two centers to smaller neighbors where liberalism also lagged: Korea, Vietnam, and Eastern Europe. The first great era of expansion of the pure socialist system ended with its first overseas victory, the Cuban revolution of 1959, a mere ninety miles from the United States.

In the 1920s, a different kind of socialism arose in Japan, Italy, and Germany, with disastrous results. In "national" socialism most business remains in private hands, but the government directs it to serve the nation. In Japan and Germany especially, the "nation" meant "race" in a narrow sense: the Germanic race or the Japanese race. The term *Nazi* is short for "national socialist" in German. In Japan's conquest of Korea in 1910 and eastern China in the 1930s, Japanese businesses replaced Chinese and European businesses there. In the German conquest of central Europe in the 1930s and 1940s, German businesses replaced Jewish, French, English, Polish, Czech, and any other business. World War II came to a peak, and then to an end, when the liberal and pure socialist worlds joined together in common cause to defeat the national socialists.

Although wiped out in Japan, Italy, and Germany, national socialism has survived in milder forms elsewhere. For example, the Ba'ath party of Iraq or Syria, the Franco regime of Spain, the National Party of South Africa, and Peronism in Argentina are forms of national socialism. The idea that the party in power directs the business sector for the benefit of some particular group of people has remained just as strong as the pure socialist idea of eliminating the business sector completely. Ba'athists want only Arab business, not English, French, or Jewish. Peronists want only Argentine business, not Spanish or English or American. South African Nationalists want only Afrikaner business, not English or Indian or black African. And so on across the world.

Milder aspects of national socialism appear in just about every country on earth. It combines the world's oldest economic form—the tribal system—with the business sector. In tribal warfare, one tribe seizes the next tribe's wealth and distributes it among its own people. In its milder form, you exclude members of other tribes from farming your land, marrying your sons or daughters, or doing business of any kind on your soil. From inside the tribe, it looks fair. Immigration policies across the world are the simplest place to find a mild version of national socialism in action, where every government seeks to restrict some benefits of the country to some definition of "us." As a full economic system national socialism has mostly died out, but in mild form and bits and pieces you can find it just about everywhere.

World War II gave way to the Cold War, an ongoing rivalry between liberalism and pure socialism. Into the 1970s, it seemed like a permanent condition. Then Mao Zedong died in 1976, and Deng Xiaoping succeeded him two years later. Deng said that he and his generation had become pure socialists in their youth because they truly believed that it would lead to greater prosperity for their people. That was the 1920s. Fifty years later, in the 1970s, it was obvious to him they were wrong. Right across his border was the starkest case: The pure socialism of North Korea led to poverty, while the business system of South Korea led to prosperity.

Deng did not legalize private business overnight. Instead he began moving away from pure socialism by loosening the constraints on the business sector. He let farmers grow crops on private plots alongside the communal fields, and let them sell their crops in town rather than hand them over to the government agency that distributes food. In 1979 he began to set up special economic zones in the south and east where foreign businesses could come in and operate by themselves, as joint ventures or partnerships with Chinese. Chinese companies were free to start up alongside them, although they were owned at first by local governments or collectives. In those areas our ten *Doing Business* indicators went from very low to fairly high scores. In 1992, Deng took a tour of the zones to see the results. Official income statistics showed what was obvious to any visitor: The business sector had brought much greater mass prosperity than China had ever known. Deng declared the experiment a success. The rest of the country followed suit. From then on China boomed.

In India a mild form of national socialism ruled after independence in 1947. The "nation" was local Indian versus foreign English. Then Pakistan split off, in true national socialist form, as a separate Islamic nation. The Indian government then imposed restrictions on Indian business that took pure socialism as far as possible without completely eliminating the business sector. A License Raj (*raj* means "regime" in Hindi) decided how many cars to produce, of what kind, with what technology, and for what price. Then it issued a small number of licenses to Indian firms to produce them, with how many workers, at what wage, with what benefits. As in China, the party in power believed this system would bring prosperity to the country. But through the 1980s the hoped-for prosperity still had not arrived. India remained very poor.

Manmohan Singh became India's finance minister in 1991, and like Deng Xiaoping he set out to turn his country from pure socialism to business. Singh eliminated the License Raj and worked to reform other elements of *Doing Business* as well. It worked. In 2004, he became prime minister. Per capita income in India went from $1,400 in 1990 to $3,800 in 2007. China's per capita income went from $1,300 in 1990 to $7,700 in 2007. A fifth of the population of the two countries rose out of poverty in that period. Their combined population is 2.5 billion, so half a billion people rose out of poverty. That means India and China together brought more people out of poverty, faster, than anywhere else on earth.

India lags China for historical reasons. For example, only 40 percent of Indians speak the main language, Hindi, and there are a dozen other major languages. In China, 90 percent of the population speaks Chinese. That helps make literacy lower in India (60 percent) than in China (90 percent), because education is so much more difficult. And democracy in India makes it harder for the government to reform quickly than in single-party China. And less than 5 percent of China is in the tropics, versus more than 50 percent for India: Agriculture is much harder to commercialize in the tropics than in the cooler temperate zone. India has farther to go than China to bring all its people out of poverty, but both countries are clearly on the right track.

Russia and Eastern Europe have also switched from pure socialism to business since the fall of the Berlin wall in 1989. These countries were much farther ahead than China and India to begin with, thanks to the greater natural endowment of Europe and their pre-socialist decades as part of the European business system. Because of this head start, progress in Russia and Eastern Europe has been less dramatic than in China and India. Most of these countries revived their business sectors by moving up the *Doing Business* rankings, but at varying speeds. Estonia ranked highest among them in 2008, ranking seventeenth out of 178 countries. Estonia's per capita income went from $7,700 in 1990 to $20,300 in 2007. In contrast, Ukraine in 2008 still ranked only 139th out of 178 countries in *Doing Business*. Its per capita income grew only from $7,200 in 1990 to $7,800 in 2007.

Beyond Europe, in recent years Vietnam has also moved up in the rankings, from pure socialism on the Chinese model to rank 91st in 2008 in *Doing Business*. Its per capita income rose from $930 in 1990 to $3,100 in 2007. Other reformers include Turkey, Jordan, Brazil, and Malaysia— and the list grows longer every year. Around the world, the alternatives to the business sector have slowly played themselves out. The other systems have failed to bring prosperity: the tribalism that once covered the whole world, the despotism of ancient Egypt and China, the feudalism of medieval Europe, the pure socialism of Russia and its imitators, the national socialism of Germany and Japan that led to World War II. Instead, the business sector has steadily grown to bring prosperity to more and more of the world's people. From Mesopotamia to Rome, to Venice, to Amsterdam, to London, to New York, to Beijing, to New Delhi, to Ho Chi Minh City—in country after country, the business sector has won the day.

Except in the poorest countries. There remains a vast swath of the modern world where the business sector still lags. A few of these countries are holdouts of the pure socialist system, such as North Korea, Cambodia, Laos, and Cuba. But most of these poor countries are in Africa, and have received vast amounts of aid from the liberal business countries. Most of the non-African countries on the list, such as Haiti and Bangladesh, follow a similar pattern: very poor, and lots of aid. Now that we know how prosperity came to other countries, we seek to understand why these poorest countries have failed to prosper despite the aid that the liberal business countries gave them.

At the start of this chapter we saw from *Doing Business* that governments of these poor countries put severe restrictions on their business sector. We want to know why they do that, despite the same evidence that convinced Deng Xiaoping to liberate business in China. Is there something about these countries that makes them different? And we want to know whether decades of foreign aid have helped or hurt the business sectors in these countries. Should rich countries increase, decrease, or change the kind of foreign aid they give to these lagging countries?

To answer these questions the next chapter looks in greater detail at the story of thwarted prosperity in these poor countries from 1960 through the present. We will find that, as elsewhere in the world, the business sector there met opposition from competing systems. In these poor countries, a mix of all these competitors played a key role: tribal, despotic, feudal, pure socialist, and national socialist systems combined. And we see the emergence of a new competitor: the aid system itself. Against this daunting array of contenders the business system lost out.

3

BUSINESS LAST

The Roots of Failure in Poverty Aid

I n 1960 Rome hosted the Summer Olympics. The closing ceremony took place on September 11, and the final results shook the world. The medal count was 103 for the Soviet Union and 71 for the United States. In gold medals the Soviet Union won forty-three and the United States took thirty-four. In the previous thirteen Olympics the host nation had won five times, because it fielded far more athletes. The United States won the other eight times. The 1960 victory by the Soviet Union was the first time a country other than the host or the United States won the Summer Olympics.

In the world press it was a victory not just for a country but for an economic system. At the time of the Russian Revolution in 1917, Russia was a poor country. In just a few years it advanced so quickly it defeated the great German military machine in World War II, launched the first satellite into space in 1957, and now eclipsed the world's biggest business sector in the eyes of the whole world.

It is easy to look back now and see that the Soviet system was doomed to fail. But in 1960 it was not so obvious. It was a long two decades later that Deng Xiaoping switched sides. In the late 1950s and through the 1960s, Europe gave independence to its overseas colonies in Latin America, Africa, and Asia, and most of these nations looked to Russia for their own path to prosperity. Few of them adopted the pure socialist system, but they took enough of its elements to cripple their local business sectors.

At the same time, most of these nations accepted aid from the liberal business countries: Europe, the United States, and later Japan. Many of the countries formally declared themselves members of the Non-Aligned Movement, founded by Nehru of India in 1955, which took neither side in the Cold War. One of the African non-aligned leaders was Julius Nyerere of Tanzania, who declared in his Arusha Declaration in 1967 an African form of socialism, which he translated as *Ujamaa* in the Swahili language. It included collective villages, along the lines of collective farms in China and Russia. Rich countries funded Ujamaa, especially through the World Bank and the national agencies of Britain, Sweden, Holland, and West Germany. Trained professionals from those agencies went to Tanzania to help design and run it.

Surely this was an odd marriage: pro-business countries giving aid to socialist ones? This is the first mystery we need to unravel in the recent history of poor countries. There are several reasons why such a marriage lasted longer than anyone might expect.

First, the on-field competition of the 1960 Olympics was a safer alternative to nuclear war. Aid competition played a similar role. The liberal business countries gave aid to prevent a country from accepting Russian military bases, from voting with Russia in the United Nations, or from trading exclusively with Russia and its allies. In the realpolitik of the Cold War, you gave aid to influence a poor country's foreign policy. You cared much less what they did with their internal policies, socialist or not.

Second, there was a great deal of support for moderate socialist policies within the liberal business countries, especially the two biggest colonizers, Britain and France. The British Labour government of 1945 to 1951 moved large portions of the economy, including the Bank of England and the iron and steel industry, from the hands of private business into government ministries. France followed a similar but lesser trend at around the same time. Britain reversed these policies only in the early 1980s, with excellent results: U.K. per capita income rose from $8,500 in 1980 to $25,000 in 2000. France went back and forth, with more nationalizations in the early 1980s. There were strong socialist parties in every country of liberal Europe. Sympathy for socialism spread easily to foreign aid, where "helping poor people" rather than "making money" seemed a noble career. The result was that government officials on both ends of aid—giving and receiving—favored a similar system.

Third, leading economists in the liberal business countries sanctioned socialist systems. For example, the German economist Wassily Leontief won the Nobel Prize in 1973 for his input-output models that showed how changes in one economic sector affected changes in another. It worked the same for a business or socialist system, for a rich country or a poor one. One of his American students, Robert Solow, won the Nobel Prize in 1987 for his growth models that showed how varying inputs of capital, labor, and technology yielded different rates of growth. Again, it made no difference if it was a business or socialist economy. Arthur Lewis won the Nobel Prize in 1979 for his work on surplus labor that industry soaks up, once again independent of the economic system. He served as an advisor to Ghana's state takeover of its business sector by its first president, Kwame Nkrumah. The key works of Leontief, Solow, and Lewis date from the 1950s and 1960s. They and other system-neutral economists influenced generations of aid professionals up to the present day.

Fourth, socialism in poor countries solved a practical problem for aid officials. Working out a single budget for a single government ministry was much easier than figuring out how to deliver a multitude of projects to a multitude of sites all over the country. Starting in 1928, Russia's central planning agency, Gosplan, produced five-year plans for government spending in every sector. Aid officials encouraged poor countries to do the same. It was a simple matter to include in their five-year plan the portion of the government budget to come from foreign aid. Problem solved. India led the way with its first five-year plan in 1950, Ghana followed in 1951, and by 1970 it was rare to find a country receiving aid without such a plan. Hollis Chenery promoted this kind of planning for aid as a key official at the U.S. Agency for International Development—USAID—in the early 1960s, and then as a vice president of the World Bank in the 1970s. These are the two biggest aid agencies, and once they adopt a common practice the smaller agencies follow along.

These four reasons explain why the liberal business countries tolerated or even promoted the use of their aid for anti-business systems in poor countries. We also need to know why the poor countries themselves favored socialism over liberalism, despite strong evidence that a thriving domestic business sector is the best path to prosperity. The Russian victory at the 1960 Olympics certainly helped. Beyond the fanfare, we can find another four reasons within the poor countries for the rise of anti-business systems.

The first reason is national socialism. The new governments in the foreign colonies aimed to favor their own people over foreigners on their soil. The end of colonialism left large numbers of English, French, Portuguese, Spanish, Dutch, Belgian, and German colonists in the new nations. They arrived through conquest, started businesses, and as of 1960 accounted for most of the local business sector. As independence neared, political parties in the colonies competed for favor among the local population by promising to shift the wealth of the country from foreign to local hands.

But if the government did so as just a one-time seizure to distribute the businesses to private citizens, the foreigners would simply buy them back. Instead, the government nationalized many of the businesses, wholly as state corporations or partially as para-statals with some shares owned by foreigners or local citizens. In this way the government took control and ran them like state agencies. It filled jobs in those businesses in the same way it filled its regular civil service. And you needed a whole range of restrictions on business to prevent foreigners from taking over the economy again. Miles of red tape for all kinds of transaction gave the government power at every step to make sure jobs and income went to its own people and not foreigners.

National socialism—favoring Africans over non-Africans—solved the problem of who benefited from the economy. In Africa especially, Europeans were not the only non-Africans. There was another category of foreign business to deal with: the Indians, Lebanese, and Arabs. The Indians learned European business as part of the British Empire and went to British colonies in Africa as laborers and petty traders. Over the years, they saved money and invested it wherever they could. For example, Indians arrived in Uganda as indentured laborers to build the British railway from the coast. Many stayed and opened small shops. One of the crops they bought from local farmers was cotton. Over time the Indians bought ginning equipment to process the cotton. The Lebanese learned European business as part of the French Empire and went to French colonies in Africa as traders. In Côte d'Ivoire, for example, they played a similar role for cocoa as Ugandan Indians did for cotton. The Arabs arrived in Africa in medieval times, along the east coast and south across the Sahara, as traders in all kinds of goods, including slaves. When slavery ended, many stayed on. In Tanzania, for example, they owned spice plantations on the islands of Zanzibar and Pemba.

The wave of nationalization after independence took over Indian, Lebanese, and Arab businesses too. Sometimes the resentment of their business success went even further. For example, black Africans on Zanzibar killed many Arabs during a 1964 rebellion. Most of the survivors fled the island. In 1972, the dictator Idi Amin expelled the Indians from Uganda. In many former colonies of southeast Asia, Chinese traders from British outposts on the China coast found themselves in a similar fix. In Malaysia, for example, plans to give preference to Malays in government jobs led Singapore to secede in 1965, because of the many overseas Chinese there. Vietnam expelled overseas Chinese in the late 1970s.

The new governments of poor countries in the 1960s, and the people themselves, blamed all these foreigners for making them poor. They claimed that national socialism, usually in combination with some form of pure socialism, was a fair and effective means to repair the damage of

European colonialism and the shady practices of Indian, Lebanese, Arab, or Chinese merchants. But they were wrong in both their diagnosis and their remedy. The two main colonial powers, Britain and France, brought a version of their liberal business systems to their colonies. In Africa especially, over the main colonial period from 1900 to 1960 they brought more prosperity than the continent had ever seen. In Ghana, for example, the Organization for Economic Cooperation and Development (OECD) estimates per capita income in constant dollars as $462 in 1870 and $1,122 in 1950. Roads, railways, ports, schools, hospitals, factories, cash crops: For the most part these all came first to Africa during the colonial period. As of 1960, Africa was behind Europe but ahead of the Africa of 1900.

At first, Europeans did not bring prosperity. They brought the slave trade, a great evil, but that preceded the colonial era. And Belgium's King Leopold brought slavery back to Congo in the first decade of the twentieth century, but otherwise the main period of colonial rule came after the slave trade ended. The British and French did practice forced labor in their colonies, for Africans unable to pay their taxes in money. But by 1900, Britain and France were already liberal countries. That spared their colonies the oppression and violence of less liberal colonial masters, such as the feudal Spanish or Portuguese in Africa and Latin America, or the national socialist Germans and Japanese before and during World War II.

These different forms of colonialism produced different results in the colonies. The more liberal the colonial master, the more the colony prospered. India, Ireland, Hong Kong, and the American states were British colonies for far longer than any of Africa, while Britain itself was struggling to move from feudalism to business. For these colonies the benefit of the British business system outweighed in the end the harm of the British feudal system. Ancient Gaul—modern France—thrived as a Roman colony. It may seem only natural to blame colonialism for Africa poverty. But in throwing out the bathwater of foreign rule, the new nations of Africa threw out the baby too—the business system within it.

Cheating by foreign traders as an explanation for poverty has an even older lineage than blaming colonialism. It's that ancient resentment of the local farmers who see that the miller who buys their grain is richer than they are. He must be cheating. Although some of these foreigners intermarried with Africans, most did not. That added to the resentment, for the Africans saw the foreigners keeping all the profit for themselves. There is some truth to this, for good reasons. It takes at least a generation of education to learn the language, techniques, and habits of business. And most small businesses are run by a family. As your children grow old enough to marry, you look for a match that's good for business. The best match is a fellow trading family that speaks the same language as you do and is as prosperous as you are or more so. It's a version of the same tribal networks that persist among Africans for similar reasons, as we will soon see.

A second reason the new governments of poor countries favored socialism over business was the dream of technology. Sputnik in 1957 showed the world that the Soviet Union had better science than the liberal business countries. And science met central planning in the Soviet triumph of World War II: Gosplan defeated the Germans with the T-34 tank. When Lenin took over in 1917, German industry dwarfed Russia's. Germany conquered Europe and invaded Russia with the best arms in the world. Under Stalin's Gosplan, Russian industry geared up to design the best tank in the world and produce it in greater numbers than any other tank in history. Soviet industrial technology, harnessed through central planning, saved the world from the Nazis.

After 1960, most poor countries set out to industrialize in the same way. In the liberal business countries, industrialization took centuries. In Russia central planning did it in decades. It was simply a matter of government officials applying the best technology to every sector of the economy. The expense was high, but that's where foreign aid came in. A few short decades of capital investment, and poor countries would catch up with the liberal business countries just like Russia did. If left to the liberal business sector, it would take too long. People were poor. They needed to rise from poverty quickly.

There are three distinct fallacies in this single dream of industrial technology solving the problem of poverty. The first fallacy is the power of science per se: Put in place the best technology, because that's the source of prosperity. Isn't that how it worked in Europe: first the scientific revolution, then the industrial revolution that applied science to industry? The answer is: Not quite. It's the other way around. The industrial revolution began in England around 1800. We have traced the growth of the business sector from Sumer to Rome to Venice to Amsterdam to London: The rise of the business system was the key that made the industrial revolution possible. The leap to industry owed little or nothing to scientific discovery. Arkwright's power loom and Whitney's cotton gin worked by mechanics that the ancient Greeks and Chinese already knew. Murdock's gas light used knowledge from ancient Persia.

As the industrial revolution gained steam in the nineteenth century, the new prosperity it brought to the overall economy of Europe and the United States gave scientists the luxury of devoting time to commercial science. The industrial revolution was well under way by the mid-1800s, when the first new advances came in electricity and chemicals. That led to more prosperity, which led to more science. You can get science by other means, as in the Soviet Union, by simple government spending. But Sputnik shows that scientific success does not lead to prosperity. The Soviet Union did have excellent science. But it had no business system. That was the problem.

The second fallacy of industrial technology leading to prosperity is the role of industry itself. Here too leading economists played a key role in the mistake. Our Nobel laureates Leontief, Solow, and Lewis differed in many details, but they all agreed that economic growth came from moving people from agriculture to industry. So the faster you do that, the faster you reach prosperity. A socialist system can do that faster than a business system, as Russia showed so dramatically. You do it by government decree. But again, in successful economies it actually worked the other way around. The history of prosperous countries shows that the business system exploits opportunity when and where it can. All human society was rural at some point, and in most cases prosperity came first from commercial farming and then from industry. Dutch agriculture was the first domestic business to prosper. The same was true for England. When Deng Xiaoping allowed business in China, farming was the first business that masses of Chinese turned to. And it worked.

The third fallacy of industrial technology is the means of delivery: central planning. Technical experts decide what technology goes where, that goes into the budget, and the government agency delivers it. Problem solved. But that is not how the industrial revolution worked. Business exploited whatever technology existed, in whatever sector it could. Scientists and inventors then saw the financial benefit of further technology in those sectors, for products that business used. Central planning stifles incentive for the advance of technology, because it prevents research from following opportunities as they arise and change. Instead, scientists work on what the planners tell them to.

Technology increases productivity dramatically, and that leads to greater prosperity, but only if people use the technology, and only if business has the means to get the right technology into the hands of the right people, because they're willing to buy it. Since 1980 especially, technology businesses have taken off in prosperous countries, so we understand well now the connection between business and technology. But before that, in the 1960s and 1970s, central planning gave poor countries hope that they could quickly harness science and catch up with the rest of the world.

These first two reasons that poor countries turned anti-business—to favor local over foreign and the dream of technology—dwell in the realm of high-level policy. The government has the power to reverse the error. Our next two reasons reveal why the governments of poor countries did not want to reverse these errors. National socialism and pure socialism, forced industrialization, and central planning are bad enough, but aid also helped maintain tribalism and despotism in poor countries. These two are business's oldest enemies, and the hardest to defeat.

Let's take tribalism first. Remember that the whole world was tribal at some point. Like poverty, tribalism is part of the original human condition. In the purest form of tribalism, you care only about your family, your family's family, your neighbors, your neighbor's family, and so on, in a complex web that touches dozens, or hundreds, thousands, or millions, depending on the size of your tribe. This is the web of reciprocity: You favor members of your tribe because they are more likely to favor you in some way, through marriage or money or some kind of help, next week or ten years down the road. Tribalism is not an irrational emotion. It's a practical economic system, an ancient fact of life that remains strong to the present day.

The most common marker of tribe is language. There are still more than six thousand languages spoken on earth. At least as many have died out through the ages. Race or physical type is another common marker of tribe, but there are far fewer physical types on earth than different languages. In most cases neighboring tribes look similar, so language makes far more difference than physical appearance. Religion is a third common marker. About a dozen religions embrace more than one language, and countless religions are specific to one language group. There are fewer than 200 countries on earth, so the average country today has dozens of languages—that is, dozens of tribes—within its borders.

Africa especially has more tribes per capita than anywhere else on earth. There are about 2,000 African languages, with 300,000 speakers each. There are about fifty African countries, so each country has an average of forty languages. In ancient times all parts of the world were like Africa is today. As kingdoms and empires grew, one language spread across the realm. For example, at the time of the French Revolution, only a quarter of the current area of

France spoke French as a first language. Today nearly 100 percent speak French.

Large, long-lasting kingdoms like France were few and far between in the history of sub-Saharan Africa. So there was little chance for one language—one tribe—to prevail over many others. The result was that a multitude of tribes persisted rather than give way to one larger tribe. One reason for this is natural poverty. Empires that impose a single language typically start from a wealthier region conquering poorer ones. This is true for despotic empires like ancient Egypt and China that began in fertile river valleys. And it's true for the modern colonial empires of prosperous European nations like Britain and France. Vast stretches of Africa were so naturally poor that there was nowhere for an empire to start. In the absence of an enduring empire, a multitude of small tribes endure instead.

Geography makes some countries poorer than others, and less able to escape poverty once the business system arrives there. Although all the world started out poor, and the spread of the business system brought the chance for prosperity to place after place, geography made it easier or harder to take advantage. Around 1000 A.D., the Arab Empire was more prosperous than the Holy Roman Empire, because it preserved more of the old Roman business system. But once the business system took hold in northern Europe, geography helped it leap ahead even faster. Most of the farmland the Arab empire covered is very poor. Most of farmland of northern Europe is very rich.

The three basic pillars of geographic advantage for business success are farming, minerals, and water transport. The plains and valleys of the temperate zone, especially 30 to 50 degrees from the equator, have the best farming conditions for commercial agriculture. Temperatures are low enough to kill off most plant and animal diseases, especially if there is a winter frost, and to rot plant matter slowly enough in the soil to leave plenty of nutrients for crops to grow. And as luck would have it, most of those temperate regions have young soil left by recent uplifting of mountains, inland lakes, or flooding rivers. This fortunate temperate band includes the United States, Europe, China, and Japan. Prosperity is easier there thanks to this basic geography. In some parts of the tropics, such as Southeast Asia, fertile river valleys and volcanic soils make for good farming. But most of the tropics have ordinary upland soil, and farming there is poor.

As for minerals, these appear in many places all over the earth. When you find them near temperate farmland, they integrate nicely into your business system. Leading examples of countries with this happy combination of circumstances are the United States, Canada, Australia, China, England, France, and Germany. They have temperate farmland and mineral wealth. All of these countries have iron and coal, which makes steel, thereby permitting the manufacture of tractors and trucks and other equipment that help farming become a big business. Steel allows the building of factories and machinery for industry, and farms

provide the basic chemicals and raw materials for countless industrial products. If you then have oil or copper or
other industrial minerals, the result is a balanced business
system of country and city combined.

When you find minerals without temperate farmland,
it's harder to develop a full business system, as mining
companies simply export the minerals. Or the government
claims the minerals by right, forms its own company to ex-
ploit them, and absorbs the revenue into its budget. Most
Arab and African oil countries fit one or both of these pat-
terns. Russia has temperate farmland and minerals but is
still struggling to develop a full business system from its
heritage of feudal and pure socialist systems.

The third geographic advantage, water transport, makes
the whole business system better. Long, wide, slow rivers
that ships can enter from sea are best. If those rivers flow
from temperate farmland, even better, because they then
help make a prosperous region even richer. Again, northern Europe, China, and the United States are the clearest
examples, and their main ports are at the mouths of their
great rivers, like New Orleans or Antwerp or Shanghai. Or
you find yourself at the crossroads of sea travel with a good
natural harbor, like Venice or Singapore. Japan had excellent temperate farmland and enough iron and coal for steel
to get started on local industry. When its coal and iron ran
out, its excellent harbors within range of the rest of Asia
meant the Japanese could range out and get the minerals they needed elsewhere. Unfortunately they did it by

conquest, with tragic results. But after World War II, they tried ordinary business instead, with great success.

On all three geographic counts—temperate farmland, minerals, and water transport—Africa comes up short. Take a globe or world map and place two fingers on the Tropic of Cancer and the Tropic of Capricorn. Move your fingers along the lines, across the world. The latitudes between your fingers are the tropics. Now look at the land masses between the lines. You'll see that Africa has more land in the tropics than anywhere else on earth. Plant and animal diseases thrive in the tropical heat. Plant matter decays too quickly for crops to draw out the nutrients first. As luck would have it, Africa is the oldest continent too: a vast ancient plateau worn flat from eons of erosion. There have been very few recent upliftings of land, new inland lakes, or flooding rivers to renew the soil.

There are two major exceptions. In parts of East Africa, rifts in the earth's crust threw up new valleys and volcanoes with fresh soil, high enough above sea level for cooler temperatures. You find some temperate farming there, especially in Kenya. But not much. Look on a map and you see that even there the new, higher parts are scattered islands in the vast sea of old, flat Africa. The second exception is South Africa, far enough south to be out of the tropics. There is temperate farming there too.

Most of the rest of the world's poor countries are also in the tropics. The low productivity of tropical agriculture is one of the biggest constraints on a prosperous business system there. Indonesia has volcanic soil, so that helps. Vietnam, India, and Bangladesh have flooding rivers, so that makes rice a viable commercial crop. Costa Rica and southern Brazil have wet new mountains, which is good for arabica coffee. Central Brazil has cattle and soybeans, not as stable crops but as short-term harvests from cutting new patches of rainforest every few years. Overall the tropics are poor for farming, but among tropical countries Africa is worse off than most.

As for minerals, Africa in aggregate has many. But each country has only a few, or none. The total mineral output of Africa is less than that of the United States or the former Soviet Union. Every country of Africa suffers from a lack of minerals, especially iron and coal to make steel. Instead you find one or two specialty minerals in one place. Ghana has aluminum. Zambia and Congo have copper. Nigeria and Angola have oil. When you find only one mineral and there's no temperate farmland for a local business sector, the best thing to do is export that mineral to a business sector that can use it. So Africa exports its minerals to prosperous countries elsewhere. The mining company and its employees get some benefit, and the government receives a big royalty check. There is very little ripple effect into the local business sector.

The one exception in sub-Saharan Africa is South Africa, where you find iron and coal, gold, and diamonds. Because there is temperate farmland too, all contribute to the same thriving local business system, where the business of farming spurs other kinds of business, and minerals serve them all. Zimbabwe, Botswana, and Namibia nearby are somewhat similar. All have had thriving business sectors, although Zimbabwe lately has taken a turn for the worse. We shall see in a moment why.

Last but not least, Africa suffers from poor transport. It does have long, flat rivers, like the Congo and the Niger. But the ancient plateau of Africa rose up as a unit many ages ago, to now sit just a bit above sea level. That means that as a ship heads from the sea up an African river, it soon encounters rapids or waterfalls that block further passage. If you start from the other end and follow an African river toward the sea, you can go a long way along the wide, flat channel, but then you reach that same waterfall or set of rapids from the other side. You can't reach the sea. In contrast, the great rivers of China, Europe, and North America, and even the Amazon of Brazil, lead smoothly from far inland all the way to the sea.

The absence of river transport to the sea also means that Africa lacks a river seaport like New Orleans or Shanghai. Africa's coastline has very few bays and harbors for natural ports like Singapore. Look on the map and you'll see Africa's smooth shape, unlike the ragged edges of Europe and the east coast of the United States. Two exceptions are Dakar, Senegal, on the western tip of the continent, and Cape Town, South Africa, on the southern tip. Both have deep, sheltered harbors and good locations on major shipping routes around the continent.

The drier, flat parts of tropical Africa are good for roads and railways. The wetter parts, as in most of the tropics, are bad. Rain washes away the roads and railbeds. Yet the drier parts tend to be farther inland, so to reach them from the sea you have to go through the wet parts. And because of Africa's width west to east, the distances to the sea are very great. South Africa again is a lucky exception, where the continent narrows to a point at the tip.

This basic geographic poverty of Africa explains in large part the persistence of tribal systems there. You leave your tribal world when a better one appears, or someone forces you to switch. The poverty of Africa made it the last one conquered by bigger empires of any kind, African or foreign. Large medieval Africa kingdoms like Songhai or Luba-Lunda were never prosperous enough to take much territory for long enough to absorb many tribes. The closest an outside empire came was that of the Arabs after 700 A.D. They conquered North Africa in only a decade, but that was by horse, north of the tropics. When they crossed the Sahara to the tropical savannah, they found a narrow band dry and cool enough for horses. But the land was poor. Farther south, the hotter, wetter climate killed their horses. So they turned back. Local Africans took up horses and conquered across that narrow band. But they too could never go south to the rest of Africa. Centuries later Dutch sailors rounded Africa's southern tip to find that the temperate land there supported horses. That land became South Africa.

Centuries of poverty in Africa, with little conquest by outsiders or insiders, meant that each tribe had time to master its local territory. The vast African plateau is a patchwork of microclimates where the soil is a little better here, rainfall is a little more reliable there, you get seasonal pools for livestock to drink somewhere else. Each tribe developed elaborate methods of raising crops or livestock to get the most out of its difficult land. And each tribe developed elaborate arrangements of distributing harvests or newborn livestock to blood kin, chiefs, and in-laws, so that if one year my crop fails, I will get some of yours. And if yours fails, you get some of mine. Or the chief will give some of his. And so on through the tribe.

This tribal system carried over into modern jobs in independent Africa. Under African socialism most governments expanded quickly, to run factories, ports, railroads, schools, hospitals, farms, buses—to varying degrees, the entire economy. The government hired people to fill these jobs. If you had the power to hire, you looked first to your tribe, for the same reasons as always: You might not have that job forever, and if you lose it your tribe will help you. So you hire from your tribe. Then when money comes into your government budget, or someone pays fees to your office, you take some of that money and give it to members of your tribe, for the same reason. With many tribal connections to feed, you take as much as you can.

This kind of petty corruption has always existed whenever a government has handled money of any kind. From ancient Mesopotamia to every country on earth today some percentage of government revenue always disappears. The only effective antidote is a business middle class, where the majority of people think that they will do better if the system works properly than if everyone steals what they can. An ineffective antidote is an iron hand, where government spies and police watch everyone closely and punish severely whomever they catch. National socialist and pure socialist governments have tried this and failed, including Nazi Germany and the Soviet Union. Whoever runs the spies and police becomes corrupt, and that can be even worse.

In the early days of African independence, tribal corruption took over quickly. In Nigeria the great writer Chinua Achebe told the tale with his two great novels of the period, *No Longer at Ease* and *A Man of the People*. In both stories we see upstanding young men in government jobs who try to resist the pressure from family and tribe to turn corrupt and send money back home to support their home villages. The tales are tragedies: Corruption wins. You see the same trend in other poor countries of that time. Africa stands out simply because it is the biggest and poorest. But the problem is the same. A large share of the government budget after independence, including aid, trickled down to a vast population through widespread petty corruption. The previous tribal system was the mechanism of flow.

Witness what happens at a border crossing, let's say between Côte d'Ivoire and Burkina Faso, and what the border guards do. First we might wonder why there is a border there at all. The colonial powers found thousands of separate tribes and threw them together into larger territories—but not large enough. Côte d'Ivoire and Burkina Faso together have more than 100 tribes who total 33 million people, in a combined area of 230,000 square miles. For comparison, Texas has 23 million people in 330,000 square miles. The combined size of these two economies is $50 billion per year, about the same as that for Texas's third biggest city, San Antonio, with a million people. But San Antonio has the benefit of no border through town, no border with the rest of Texas, and no border with all the other American states. Surely Burkina Faso and Côte d'Ivoire would both benefit from being one country, not two. Fewer borders makes more economic sense. But only if you already have a business system. In a tribal system, the more borders, the better.

To see why, let's watch the border guards in action. A bus arrives, to cross from Burkina to Côte d'Ivoire. It stops at the Burkina guard post. Everyone gets off and lines up. One by one the passengers hand over their identification papers for inspection. Folded into each document is a 500 franc note, about one U.S. dollar. The guard takes it and hands back the document. Twenty passengers, twenty dollars. The bus driver gives a 5,000 franc note, or $10. Thirty dollars total. Six guards, $5 each. Everyone gets back on the bus. A few yards away on the Côte d'Ivoire side, the guards do the same thing. Five buses a day makes $25 per day per guard. Each one works six days out of seven, so that's $150 per guard per week, or $7,500 per year.

The governments of Côte d'Ivoire and Burkina Faso pay their border guards very little. But having them on the payroll means that someone gets to hire them, and so do a favor for a tribal member. The more borders, the more border guards. Each border guard gives half the money to his boss. His boss gives half the money to his boss. Of the money the border guard keeps—$3,750 per year—he sends a fifth to his wife back in their village, a fifth to his cousin who is taking care of the guard's two children while they go to school in a bigger town, a fifth to his mother and father in a different village, and a fifth to a cousin to pay off a loan when the guard was sick for a year with pneumonia. Each person the guard sends money to uses much of it in turn to feed, clothe, house, or otherwise aid other members of the tribe.

The guard ends up keeping $750 per year for himself. By the standards of prosperous countries today, our guard is still poor. And he has done much good for many people. Yet a hundred strangers a day hate him for stealing their money. But what else can he do? Where else will he get $150 per week? And the passengers on the bus in turn receive some kind of benefit from relatives working in some other government job, at a port or factory or school. They love their own relatives who prey on others, and hate the others who prey on them.

In this kind of tribal economy the more connections you have and the more gifts you give, the more chances you have of getting gifts back, especially if someone you know gets an even better job, with more money to siphon off, so the gifts to you get bigger. It takes a kind of entrepreneurship to succeed in this system, and there is a meritocracy of sorts that rewards good planning, strategic thinking, and the social skills that help you climb the web of relations to higher income. But the overall effect is to distribute money that drains the larger economy, rather than real business transactions that create real jobs that enlarge the economy.

In this kind of tribal system, the more government jobs, the better. In Mozambique it takes twelve steps to start a business. That means you go to twelve different government offices to fill out a form. That gives a job to twelve Mozambiquans behind the desks. They get their small salary plus the bribe you give them to get their stamp on your document. Only when you have the twelve stamps can you run your business without the police shutting you down.

At the highest level this kind of tribal corruption merges nicely with national socialism. Take the case of Bolivia. In 2006, the Indian majority elected one of their own, Evo Morales, to overthrow the existing system of privilege for the Spanish minority. This problem calls to mind the 1960s in Africa. Tribalism works for the wealthy too, so the Spanish minority discriminated against Indians to keep the wealth of the country for themselves. But the answer is not to strangle the business system through national or pure socialism, but to open up the business system to Indians. This is very hard to do, especially when the majority who elected you think it's as easy as taking from the rich and giving to the poor. Few Indians have the skills to compete immediately in the normal business system. So Morales tried national socialism at the highest level: He nationalized the main industries of natural gas and mineral processing. That created more government jobs, with lots more money passing through the hands of whoever gets those jobs, and that money trickles down as tribal corruption to the lower levels.

National socialism, the dream of technology, and the enduring tribal system are all strong reasons why poor countries after 1960 strangled their business systems. The fourth and last reason is despotism. This is the oldest enemy of business, and the hardest to defeat. The kings of Mesopotamia, Egypt, and China ruled through their armies, which allowed them to seize whatever they wanted, at any time, from their own people. The tribal and feudal systems were more democratic, because chiefs or kings had to provide some benefit or else their followers would switch to somebody else. The feudal lords of England tied King John to a tree to make him sign the Magna Carta in 1215, which started the long road to parliamentary rule. John's power came from the armies of those lords, so he had to agree. Likewise, all tribes have some means of deposing a chief.

But a despot rules by force. And so poor countries have many coups. An army officer sees that the ruling despot depends on the army to stay in power, and so arranges with other officers to overthrow the despot and rule by force directly. Usually, the next step is some kind of national socialism, as in Burma, Iraq, or most of Africa. That makes the despot popular, at least for a time. When Idi Amin expelled the Indians from Uganda in 1972, most Ugandans cheered. The Sunni minority in Iraq cheered Saddam Hussein, who favored them in the economy. Despotism and national socialism go very well together, and both are bad for business. In recent years one sign of Uganda's business recovery is that some Indians have returned and revived their cotton mills.

Since 1960, many African nations have gone back and forth between elected national socialists and pure despots. For our guards on the Burkina border, nothing much changes. The biggest difference is the future of business. Bangladesh is poor and corrupt, but business can struggle along and perhaps one day win out against national socialism and tribal corruption. In Burma, army despots keep business at bay with an iron fist. They know that as soon as they open up, Chinese traders will return. Who knows what balance of power will result. Perhaps some of the generals will switch sides, but until they do, or a foreign army invades, business is doomed in Burma.

History shows that the best check on despotism is a thriving business class. This often means democracy, but not always. As of 1900 the British cabinet still looked a lot like the House of Lords, and Queen Victoria was still the official head of government. Yet the business class had won enough freedom and rights to operate without harm or fear. No one knows if China will become a democracy, but already we see that the new business class is the only effective check on government power.

African countries have the weakest business classes in the world. Even one of its strongest, in Zimbabwe, has recently lost out to the despotism of Robert Mugabe. At independence in 1980, Mugabe chose a mild form of national socialism, but that failed to bring enough prosperity, fast enough, to his target tribes. It is usually a coup or an election that makes the change between national socialism and outright despotism. A new leader, a new system. Zimbabwe is unusual in that the same leader made the switch.

National socialism, the dream of technology, tribalism, and despotism—no wonder the business system failed to thrive in most poor countries since 1960. Unfortunately, aid only added fuel to the fire. At first it came in simply as extra funds for the governments to expand. Especially in former colonies, a small colonial staff gave way to a lavish central government. The new president or prime minister set out to hire a cabinet of ministers, who in turn hired heads of departments, who in turn hired staff for posts in different regions of the country. Most countries quickly had a ministry of finance, a ministry of education, a ministry of agriculture, a ministry of mines, a ministry of commerce, a ministry of defense, a ministry of justice, a ministry of transport, a ministry of trade, a ministry of fisheries, a ministry of health, a ministry of foreign affairs, a ministry of labor, a ministry of energy, a ministry of forestry, and so on.

Aid paid for most or sometimes all of this expansion. Whenever the local government or aid agencies came up with a new problem, you saw a new ministry to handle it: the ministry of women's affairs, the ministry of the environment, the ministry of housing, the ministry of science and technology, the ministry of tourism. The capital and the countryside filled with civil servants, who either siphoned off their own budgets or demanded bribes, like our guards at the border between Côte d'Ivoire and Burkina Faso. Most of the corruption happened well out of direct view of the aid agencies, but they did notice the waste and corruption. The plans they funded—this many acres planted with improved seeds distributed by that many government extension agents—did not happen as they planned. So they sent in technical experts from their own countries to work alongside the ministry staff, and set up special project teams independent of direct ministry control. But that didn't work either. Waste, corruption, and poverty persisted.

Until China began its reforms and the Berlin wall fell in 1989, the failure of aid to bring prosperity to poor countries was lost in the noise of politics. At very least, aid bought allies in the Cold War. But in the 1990s, critics of aid arose in the donor countries. They pointed out that the target countries were still very poor. What good did all that aid do?

The aid system gave three answers. First, it said that aid for education, health, water, ports, and roads provided the basic infrastructure for economic growth. Prosperity will follow, but not right away. Europe took centuries to prosper. Poor countries need vast amounts of aid for decades to bring the people and the transportation system up to a basic level. Second, it admitted that local corruption stole much of the money, so the answer was tighter controls on corruption. Third, it said that until democracy arrives in these countries, the government will stay corrupt. So nongovernmental agencies should handle the aid instead.

For the most part these answers worked, in that they won for the aid system another decade of life. Yet all three answers are wrong. Again, they have it all backward. Let's take a look at these three fallacies in turn.

In prosperous countries a thriving business system came first, and that system provided the taxes to improve public education, health, water, ports, and roads. If you try to skip ahead and build these things first, you must have a government or NGO bureaucracy to do it. If you look at prosperous countries, you find many businesses that make up the education, health, water, port, and road systems, directly or indirectly. For example, private businesses make the equipment that a public hospital uses. In this way public spending can help the business sector: The more public hospitals, the more equipment they buy. But in the absence of a thriving domestic business sector and without reform of the ten elements of *Doing Business*, spending money on public works only compounds the problem.

The second fallacy, anti-corruption, puts a band-aid on a dying patient. Corruption is an enduring problem for governments of all kinds, from ancient Mesopotamia to rich countries today. It will always be with us, and we must always fight it. But our strongest weapon against it is a thriving domestic business sector. Think back to the 1980s, when Mikhail Gorbachev began to liberalize the Soviet Union. Would you advise an anti-corruption program to make the Soviet bureaucracy work better? Or would you want to dismantle it and let a business sector grow instead? Of course as the business sector grows, you want the same anti-corruption controls you find in prosperous countries. Yet anti-corruption first, or only, puts the cart before the horse—or worse, gets you a cart without any horse at all.

The third fallacy, NGO aid for economic development, is perhaps the hardest to see. In prosperous countries, you have a thriving NGO sector that provides a wide range of useful services, especially to the poor. We have nonprofit hospitals, schools, housing, legal defense, arts, and environmental programs. Why not extend the same system to poor countries? Again, this puts the cart before the horse. A prosperous business sector provides the money for a thriving NGO sector. If your NGO sector is bigger than your business sector and you don't do the ten business reforms, the local economy is doomed.

NGOs started out on the right foot in poor countries, helping refugees from the First and Second World Wars. They came to sub-Saharan Africa in force only in the late 1960s, when severe drought made millions of refugees. To this day, NGOs do a wonderful job of refugee relief. After the droughts, the government aid system asked the NGOs to stay on and switch from relief to economic development. The NGOs made a big mistake: They said yes. And so began the era of village development projects. NGO staff members survey a village to find what people lack. They then design and fund a project to provide it: wells, schools, clinics, woodlots for firewood, food, housing, medicine, irrigation, and grinding machines for grain. The variety of NGO village development projects is truly vast.

But village development projects have consistently failed as a mechanism of economic development. The basic problem is this: When you find a need, do you "design a project" or "start a business"? These are two very different ideas, from two different worlds of action. For example, in 2006, a group of business students traveled to Kenya to help out a Millennium Development Village, the kind we met through Trinity Church in our first chapter. The Village had a technology program that designed a cheap lantern that the village could make and sell. The staff of the Village asked the business students for a marketing plan. Right away, the students found an entrepreneur nearby who sold a similar lantern for a fraction of the price. The business students proposed that the Village become a marketer of that cheaper lamp to other villages, and make a profit that way. The entrepreneur agreed. The Village technology program said no. It wanted to make and sell its own lamp.

These village development projects are the darlings of NGO aid. You can make a donation from the comfort of your home and then take a trip to visit the village well you paid for. The villagers will welcome you gladly. Nobody mentions that ten years ago there was another well somebody paid for that rusted solid after two years because nobody knew how to fix it or had the money to do so. Celebrities take these tours with cameras along, so we can all watch and then do the same ourselves. But is that the route to prosperity? Does Bono entrust his music tours or album production to NGOs? Does Angelina Jolie star in movies made by NGOs? When Bill Gates founded Microsoft, did he make it an NGO? NGOs are fine for charity, like refugee relief, but they do not provide the engine of prosperity.

These three fallacies—human and physical infrastructure first, anti-corruption, and NGO projects—kept aid alive but failed to bring prosperity. Meanwhile, there was one glaring success: microfinance. It began in one of the world's poorest countries, Bangladesh. The history of microfinance shows that aid can work in favor of the local business sector, rather than against it. Let's take a look at how microfinance arose in Bangladesh and spread elsewhere at great enough scale to create an alternative aid system.

The founder of microfinance, Muhammad Yunus, began his career as a green revolution economist. The green revolution was a technical advance that brought more food to poor countries through hybrid seeds that gave higher yields per acre, but it did not bring mass prosperity. In 1976, Yunus noticed that the poor of Bangladesh did not own enough land to take advantage of the new seeds. He surveyed a small village near his university and found that forty-six poor women needed only $22 to get out of debt for the bamboo they bought to make furniture for sale. In despair at such small-time poverty, Yunus gave them the money. To his surprise, they paid it back. He lent them more. They paid it back. So began microfinance.

Yunus had an ongoing research grant from the Ford Foundation, an American NGO, and used some of the money on the spot for that initial survey. He used more of it to pay his students as the first microfinance staff. When there were too many loans to handle alone, he got the local branch of the state-owned bank to bend its own rules and make the loans instead. State-owned banks in poor countries are typically creatures of the aid system, and here is an example of one changing its policy to do the right thing. More and more loans led Yunus to form his own bank, Grameen, and take aid money to expand. A mission from the U.N.'s International Fund for Agricultural Development had unspent funds in its budget and was looking for a way to spend the money on the green revolution in Bangladesh, and Yunus convinced them to bend their rules and fund Grameen instead. Then the MacArthur Foundation, another American NGO, funded Grameen to expand overseas.

Today there are hundreds of microfinance programs in poor countries throughout the world. Many are banks, like Grameen, and many are NGOs that run like banks. As it turns out, the NGO structure can do all sorts of things. The U.S. National Football League, for example, is an NGO. NGOs can help business, and aid can help those NGOs. But you must be choosy: Yunus turned down World Bank funding many times, because bank staff wanted to tell him what to give loans for, based on their analysis of the Bangladesh economy. They were central planners at heart and wanted to fund him to do what they planned. But Yunus insisted on letting his borrowers use the money for whatever they wanted, as long as they paid it back. Yunus runs Grameen in the same opportunistic way that businesses operate, following opportunity rather than five-year plans.

Support for microfinance is a good example of a pro-business program in development aid to poor countries. Yet it has a limit. Governments found that microfinance did not disturb the rest of the aid system. Microfinance borrowers are typically part of the informal sector: that is, they don't register their businesses or fall under any of the normal business restrictions that our ten elements track. Once a micro-business grows big enough to graduate from micro-loans to small business loans, they hit a ceiling. Now they fall under the ten elements. In that way they never grow to a normal business sector. They stay micro. The rest of the aid system can go on as before. Microfinance is still today but a tiny fraction of total aid spending. Yet its success gives us hope that aid can support business rather than suppress it.

Let's conclude our history of how and why aid failed with the latest figures from the World Bank. In August 2008, its Development Research Group reported that the percentage of the world's people living in extreme poverty fell by half from 1981 to 2005: that is, from 52 percent to 26 percent. Yet almost all that progress came in Asian countries that turned to business, especially China and India. In countries that receive aid instead, especially most of sub-Saharan Africa, the poverty rate remained unchanged over those years.

You would think that such failure would lead the aid system to rethink what it's been doing all those years. Yet the World Bank concludes from this report, "We must redouble our efforts, especially in sub-Saharan Africa." Why is it that the only thing the aid system can think of to do is more of the same, even if it doesn't work?

There are four basic reasons. We saw the first one in our very first chapter: the charity trap. There is a very human and timeless urge to give poor people whatever they lack. But if the charity system is bigger than the business system, prosperity will never come. There is a ceaseless flood of money from rich countries to poor countries for food, clothing, shelter, medicine, water, and whatever else poor people need. To divert most of that money to the business sector will take a huge shift in public awareness back in the rich countries themselves.

The second reason the aid system endures is for its own self-interest. Thousands of professionals in government and NGO agencies depend on the current aid system for their careers. University professors teach development studies to use the aid. The vast majority of these professionals are specialists in their fields: education, health, water, agriculture, and the like. They know how the government and NGO systems work to deliver aid in their field. Yet they know next to nothing about business. If aid switches to the business sector, they fear they will lose their jobs. In private many of these professionals admit to each other that the current aid system doesn't work. In public they advocate for more money to feed the aid system, in the name of the poor people they serve.

The third reason the aid system endures is the absence of advocates in rich countries in favor of the business sector in poor countries. As we saw in the struggle of business against competing systems, sympathy for pure socialism remains strong in many liberal countries. Aid provides a natural outlet for anti-business ideas because they do not disturb the politics or prosperity of the rich country itself. If you think business is a bad thing, spending public and private money from rich countries on government and NGO programs in poor countries seems like a fair and worthwhile thing to do. Even if you demonstrate that these programs don't work, some people will simply never agree to try business instead.

The last reason the aid system endures is the lack of a strong alternative means to spend vast sums of money from rich countries. We encountered this problem at the outset of the aid system in the 1960s, when one five-year government development plan was much easier to fund and administer than small bits of aid to myriad small businesses. Aid to poor countries today amounts to half a trillion dollars per year. There is no obvious way to spend that on business instead. If we know that the current aid system doesn't work, it seems cruel simply to turn our backs on poor countries and give them nothing at all.

These four reasons taken together mean that the aid system is here to stay. But there is hope. Yunus began in 1976. In 2006, he won the Nobel Peace Prize. It was a long, tough struggle. But over thirty years microfinance won out. We are fortunate that the history of aid has another major success story besides the Grameen Bank: the Marshall Plan, which revived the business sector of postwar Europe and won its founder, General George Marshall, the Nobel Peace Prize in 1953. If a Marshall Plan for poor countries starts in 2010, perhaps by 2040 it can reach the same heights as microfinance, and revive the business sector in poor countries too. The rest of this book shows how.

4

STRONG MEDICINE

The Marshall Plan as a Business Model

In previous chapters we saw how a thriving domestic business sector has stood out as the only viable path to large-scale prosperity in the history of human endeavor, how rival systems thwarted it to some degree everywhere on earth, and how the aid system adds yet another rival system that makes things even worse in the poor countries it aims to help. In the next three chapters we turn from problem to solution: how to use aid to support rather than thwart a thriving domestic business sector.

Our basic model remains unchanged: the ten elements of the World Bank's *Doing Business*. In all cases governments helped create them and helped make them work. Otherwise, competing systems—tribal, despotic, feudal, national, and pure socialism—win out instead. And over the past century especially, myriad NGOs play key roles in supporting the business sector and helping it reach as many people as possible. Chambers of Commerce are NGOs, for example, as are many business schools. Aid needs to support government agencies and NGOs as well as companies directly, but to do the right things that help rather than hinder business.

The Marshall Plan of post–World War II Europe stands out as the largest pro-business aid program in history. At the time, it was the largest aid program ever: about $20 billion per year in current dollars. This is about the same annual amount that current British Prime Minister Gordon Brown proposed for a ten-year "Marshall Plan for Africa" in 2005, when he was chancellor of the exchequer. Let's compare Brown's proposal to the original Marshall Plan, to see what it can teach us about how to help poor countries today.

Brown's plan had four main elements. First, it gave complete debt relief for loans made by rich-country governments and multilateral agencies. Second, it doubled direct development aid by rich countries, including an International Finance Facility to borrow on future promises of aid to frontload spending over a decade. Third, it committed African governments to put in place anti-corruption measures and spend more on health, education, and welfare. Fourth, it called for an end to trade barriers for African agricultural products entering rich countries.

Now let's look at the four key elements of the original Marshall Plan. First, it made large loans from the United States to European governments for restoring production. They loaned the money to private businesses, which repaid it to the local European governments. Second, each government spent the repaid funds on restoring public infrastructure to further boost production. Third, each government made pro-business policy reforms along the lines of the ten elements of *Doing Business*. Fourth, a European coordinating body reported to an American administrative body back in the United States.

We can see four striking differences between the two plans. First, Brown's version promotes charity; the original promoted business development. Second, Brown's version gives governments the lead role; the original plan gave the lead role to private businesses. Third, Brown's version mostly funds social services; the original funded business activity. The one element of Brown's plan that might help African business—ending trade barriers in rich countries on African agricultural products—does nothing for actual reform there. If a Cameroonian can't get a local license to export bananas to Britain, what difference does a lower British tariff make? Fourth, Brown's version is a list of related items for hundreds of different agencies to implement separately; the original was a single coordinated program.

Yet there are similarities too. First comes political urgency: Poor countries are in danger of social and economic collapse that can lead to violence within and across their borders, and postwar Europe was under threat of Soviet advance. Second comes speed: Brown's version aims for success in ten years, and the original lasted only four years, from 1948 to 1952. Third comes scale: As we noted, both versions total about $20 billion per year. And fourth comes commitment: Brown's version came from a genuine charitable impulse in rich countries, and the original came from American resolve against communism.

Bits and pieces of Brown's proposal found their way into the aid system. All in all, it's business as usual for aid. But a real Marshall Plan, adapted to poor countries today, would be something else entirely. We can take the core elements of the original plan and adapt them to poor countries today with the same political urgency, speed, scale, and commitment that Brown aimed for and that the original itself achieved.

Of course, poor countries today are not the same as Europe in 1948. Despite the ravages of war, Europe then was in better shape than most poor countries are now. France, for example, had a per capita income then of around $5,000 in current dollars. The only sub-Saharan African countries that are rich today are anomalies: oil-rich Gabon and Angola, and South Africa, with its temperate farmland, many minerals, and a healthy business system. And most of Europe already had a business system in place: The Marshall Plan aimed in the first instance to restore it. As we saw in earlier chapters, the poor countries of today never had such prosperity to restore. They have always been poor.

Yet as we've also seen, despite the great geographic and historical differences of countries around the world, and the different economic systems they featured—tribal, despotic, feudal, national socialist, or pure socialist—as nations become more prosperous they become more alike. Above all, they rank high on the ten elements of *Doing Business*. The normal way that people make a living is through jobs in business, and with the money they earn they pay taxes to the government that support public services, or they donate to NGOs that work on worthy causes. When he started to liberalize the Soviet Union, Mikhail Gorbachev declared, "We just want to be a normal country." The greatest hope for every poor country in the world is to become normal too.

But poor countries remain prisoners of an abnormal aid system, where government agencies and NGOs create jobs, foreign aid substitutes for tax revenue, and aid development projects substitute for the tax-spending initiatives of local, regional, and state governments. A Marshall Plan for poor countries is a big step to put poor countries on track to normal economic life.

But how? The following chapter deals with the myriad details of how a Marshall Plan might work in practice. The present chapter offers an overall picture first. It's a single picture of a single institution, versus a catalogue of the hundreds of government and NGO aid agencies active in poor countries today. For aid to support business, we need a new institution with its own large budget devoted to only that task. Otherwise, it has to fight internally with competing departments for funding and freedom of operation. Perhaps an existing aid agency can convert itself into that new institution, but even so we first need a good picture of what that new entity might be. This chapter presents how such a single agency might work today to bring business development to the poor countries of the world.

For the moment let's call this new agency simply the ECA, as in the original Marshall Plan. We don't want to call it the "World Bank," because it's not a bank and the current World Bank is a far cry from the original ECA. The World Bank is a multi-government agency that makes loans to governments for government development projects, and, increasingly, for NGO projects too. So too with its regional cousins—the Asian Development Bank, the African Development Bank, and the Inter-American Development Bank. These banks are creatures of the existing aid system and fund primarily government development projects or sometimes NGOs too. New ideas call for new institutions. The World Bank itself was new a mere sixty-three years ago.

Our new ECA works on the same business model as the Marshall Plan: It loans money to local businesses in a group of poor countries if they agree to reform their business sectors, and each national government spends the repaid loans on infrastructure to further support the business sector. Beyond these basic elements, a modern-day ECA will differ in countless details from the original version for Europe. For example, European nations already had strong business sectors, so their policy reforms under the Marshall Plan were mostly macroeconomic, to stabilize their currency and balance of payments. Most poor countries today need more basic reform to put in place the ten elements of *Doing Business*. So our new ECA would direct its energies there instead.

Like most strong medicine, this new Marshall Plan will be very hard to take. Many poor countries will say no. So too with the original Marshall Plan: The United States offered it to all of Europe, including the Soviet Union, which made sure that all of Eastern Europe under its control rejected it. The Soviets offered their own brand of economic aid instead. Sixty years later it is easy to see that the Marshall Plan helped Western Europe recover quickly and go on to decades of even greater prosperity. Eastern Europe and Russia only began to catch up in the 1990s, after they switched sides and joined the business world.

The choice for poor countries is just as stark today: Switch to business or suffer the consequences. Unfortunately, many will choose to suffer, because their leaders won't suffer at all. Aid keeps corrupt leaders rich. So the ECA can only work if donors cut off economic aid to countries who reject it. Humanitarian aid can continue, although corrupt leaders steal from that too. But the ECA would need enough funding to make the choice clear: If aid donors agree that most economic aid must go through the ECA, a poor country's total aid budget would decline if it rejected the new Marshall Plan.

Even so, it will be hard to draw the line between the two in many cases. Take food aid, for example. This began as strictly humanitarian: Drought, floods, or war prevent normal harvests, so let's bring in grain from rich countries to feed the hungry. Starting in 1954, U.S. Public Law 480 has fed billions of people with American grain. Other rich countries later followed suit. But food aid proved useful in other ways too, as a permanent subsidy to keep food prices low in poor countries. The leaders of those countries liked it because it was a cheap way to make their people happy. And aid experts thought low food prices helped industrialization by keeping factory wages low. So food aid shifted over time from sporadic and humanitarian to permanent and economic.

From a business view, food aid has not been a success. It stunts the normal development of domestic businesses that grow and sell food. Commercial agriculture has been the first step in industrialization around the world, except in the failed economies of pure socialism. So rich countries must cut food aid back to its original humanitarian use. Farmers in rich countries will object because they like the subsidy they get for producing surplus food. Governments in poor countries will object because they fix food prices and must raise them if there is less food aid, so that the poor in the cities will riot in the streets. And NGOs from rich countries now receive food aid as grants, which they "monetize" by selling the food at low prices in the poor countries where they work. The money they get pays for staff and projects. So NGOs will object too.

Food aid is just one of many puzzles the ECA must solve. Phase in business aid to the domestic food industry, and phase out economic food aid. That will help on the domestic front. As for the farmers and NGOs from rich countries, the ECA must be part of a larger campaign to sell the idea of business aid as the best way to help poor countries. The original Marshall Plan started out with only 14 percent of the American public in favor. American business leaders, through the Committee for Economic Development, ran a massive information campaign that turned the tide. Why not again? The business sector in rich countries helping the business sector in poor countries—that's surely a cause worth joining.

The next two chapters tackle these implementation problems in more detail. Here we continue to outline the basic idea of the new ECA as the main channel for economic versus humanitarian aid to poor countries. The structure of the original ECA was simple: a headquarters in Washington, a regional Organization for European Economic Co-operation (OEEC) in Europe, and small missions in every European country. The regional organization made for competition among countries: If you don't qualify for the money, a neighbor will get it. So there would be an OEEC for the Middle East (OMEEC), for West Africa (OWAEC), for the Caribbean (OCEC), and so on. Within each region, countries compete for ECA funding.

Competitive funding is already gaining ground as an idea in the aid world. The closest we come today to the original Marshall Plan is the U.S. Millennium Challenge Account (MCA). Countries must meet benchmarks for good government, social services, and economic policy to qualify. So far so good. The reward, though, is a typical government development plan. For example, Mozambique won a grant of $500 million in 2007. Some 88 percent of that goes to classic government aid projects for water, sanitation, and roads. The rest goes for government agencies to register farmland and replace diseased coconut trees. In other words, MCA funds end up in exactly the same aid system as before. The Marshall Plan, in contrast, made loans to private business as its primary activity. In postwar Europe those loans came in the form of inputs to production, such as seeds for farmers, grain for mills, lumber for construction, and machines for factories. The businesses paid their governments back in money. Our new ECA would work with money on both ends, as loans and repayment.

Yet the MCA is on the right track with competitive criteria, although there too the ECA would use a different set. As of 2008 Mozambique still ranked 134th out of 178 on the *Doing Business* list. For example, it took a Mozambiquan business 361 days and cost seven times the average income per capita to go through seventeen procedures for the government licenses it needs. In Belize, by contrast, it took sixty-six days and cost less than a fifth of average income for eleven procedures. Mozambique is still anti-business overall, and the MCA grant activities do nothing to change that. Unlike the MCA, the ECA will use a strict set of competitive criteria based wholly on *Doing Business* indicators, and ECA money will promote domestic business rather than fund traditional development projects that we know don't work.

The next question for the ECA is how to make a large number of business loans within a poor country. The biggest problem is that few of our target businesses exist yet. Microfinance funds the micro-level informal sector, while big lenders like the International Finance Corporation (IFC), a cousin of the World Bank, fund the large-scale formal sector, usually foreign. It's the missing middle—small and medium local businesses—that the ECA will help. For example, Mozambique has a microfinance bank, SOCREMO, and the IFC has funded the Dutch mining company Billiton to expand its aluminum smelting there. We saw earlier how microfinance poses no real threat to the existing aid system. And foreign firms like Billiton have an easier time operating in poor countries than domestic businesses do because they just pay a large fee to the government and pay their workers well.

Yet the ECA has much to learn from microfinance and foreign companies. Microfinance has grown so diverse over the years that you find larger business loans now too. For example, ACLEDA in Cambodia began as pure microfinance but now makes small and medium-sized business loans as well. The ECA would not make the loans directly. Instead it would look to banks that are or want to be like ACLEDA to do the actual lending.

From foreign companies we learn two main lessons, one bad and one good. Let's look at each one in turn. The bad lesson is that foreign companies are conspicuous targets of outright corruption, where government fees take the form of large bribes to government officials. In many poor countries this kind of bribery is all too common and only rarely comes to light. For example, in September 2008, a Haliburton executive pleaded guilty to paying $182 million in bribes to Nigerian officials for $6 billion in contracts for liquefied natural gas. A variant of this game is for the foreign company awarding a no-bid contract to a local company that happens to be owned by a government minister or relative to do nothing. Or to a government para-statal company, where the money flows to politicians through the normal channels of raiding the public coffers. Or the government privatizes the para-statal so that it becomes a local company owned by a government minister or relative, and that company gets the foreign contract. Under a new set of rules the ECA will help a new set of local companies comes to the fore.

As we noted before, this kind of government corruption has existed since ancient times, all over the world. The key moment is when normal business transactions finally exceed corrupt ones, a corner that India, China, and Russia appear to have turned recently but that aid countries have not. Ghana, for example, has moved up the *Doing Business* rankings from 102nd in 2006 to eighty-seventh in 2008, which is excellent progress indeed. But for the indicator "dealing with licenses," Ghana still ranked 140th out of 178 countries in 2008. There were eighteen procedures—one more than Mozambique—that took 220 days and cost 1,500 percent of average per capital income, which was twice the rate in Mozambique. Ghana has made great progress, but the road ahead is still steep.

The history of foreign companies in aid countries over the past thirty years shows clearly the danger of big bribes to government officials. When companies pay bribes, it's because if they didn't their rivals might instead and they lose out on the global competitive game. But they want to compete normally, as in their home countries. The ECA will have the effect of helping foreign companies through a new set of rules that fight this kind of corruption. But the ECA will not fund foreign firms directly. Its target is domestic firms, not foreign ones. Yet the ECA will help foreign firms indirectly, by helping create local business partners that the foreign firms now sorely lack.

Foreign companies can help domestic business directly, through ordinary business contracts, as in India, China, and Russia. For example, in early 2008, General Electric was in the last year of a contract to run an energy plant for the Indian Petrochemical Company in Gujarat. The Indian company will run it alone after that. Dell sells computers in China via Gome, a Chinese computer sales company. These contracts make business sense in the short term but also transfer business skill to the local company. The same was true of the United States in the nineteenth century, where many domestic companies first sprang up as suppliers or distributors for older and bigger European firms.

In aid countries, by contrast, you see big companies handling their own supply and distribution, even down to owning their own fleets of trucks to carry supplies from the port, their own caterers to supply meals, or their own builders to supply housing for their workers. Those should be local companies instead. The foreign firms would welcome them. The ECA will help.

The line between foreign and domestic firms will always be hard to draw. If a citizen registers a company locally but gets a salary and other funding wholly from a foreign firm, is that a local company? This gray line is one official reason for the elaborate procedures to register a company in most aid countries, to make sure that foreign wolves do not enter the country in the clothing of local sheep. The ECA, in contrast, will promote lenient rules in this regard. Witness the famous case of Bangladesh textiles, where Daewoo of South Korea opened a textile plant there, only to see Bangladeshi managers learn the trade and leave to start their own local companies. Daewoo is certainly not happy to spawn competitors, but neither are they surprised. Companies know that's always a risk of doing business, at home and abroad. Businesses copy each other all the time. It's a form of apprenticeship, which is how business has spread from the earliest days of Mesopotamia, through Rome and Venice to Holland, England, and the rest of the world.

The role of foreign business as ordinary business partner for local firms is quite different from a recent idea from C. K. Prahalad, a noted Indian scholar, that multinationals should target the "bottom of the pyramid." The millions of consumers in rich countries are the top of the pyramid, and the billions of people who live on less than $2 a day are the bottom. Foreign companies can do good and make lots of money from the bottom of the pyramid by aiming goods and services at the poor. For example, Unilever in India ran a campaign in poor villages to teach and promote handwashing, which reduced disease and sold more Unilever soap. This is certainly worthy, but it does not help local business.

Prahalad asks, "Does your business target poor people?" A better question is, "What is the effect of your business on the domestic business sector?" Unilever doing business with local Indian firms creates jobs so that people have money to buy more soap. Thankfully, India's reforms have created more Indian firms that can do business with Unilever, as suppliers of materials for their products and as sellers to Indian consumers. That's good for Indian business. If Unilever tries a handwashing campaign in Mozambique, its effect on the domestic business sector will be minimal, absent more *Doing Business* reforms.

The ECA executives must resist the pull of "bottom of the pyramid" and other programs that target poor people rather than the domestic business sector. Unilever is an especially good example because it has a wonderful reputation for "corporate social responsibility" around the world, but that is not the same thing as helping the local business.

On its Web site Unilever tells us, "In 2007, we contributed €89 million to community programmes focused on education, health, nutrition, environmental sustainability and economic development." When we look at these projects they are almost all traditional aid projects that bypass or crowd out the domestic business sector. Yet we find a few good exceptions. In India again, its Shakti project recruited and trained thousands of poor women to peddle all Unilever's household products from village to village, as microfinance entrepreneurs. That's good for Indian business. In Indonesia, Unilever actively sought out local entrepreneurs as local suppliers for their goods. That's good for Indonesian business. More typical, though, is the firm's project in Tanzania to help farmers collect the allanblackia seed that grows wild in the forest and plant it on poorer land. Unilever will buy whatever the farmers gather or reap. It certainly helps farmers to have another commercial crop, but in 2008, Tanzania ranked 170th out of 178 countries in "dealing with licenses." So no domestic company can arise as an intermediary between Unilever and the farmers. Who will play that role? The Web site tells us: "the United Nations Development Programme, international and local NGOs."

The ECA will face a blizzard of such projects that claim to promote economic development but really continue to crowd out the domestic business sector. Let's call it the "allanblackia problem": helping small farmers or entrepreneurs at the lowest level but stifling all the other domestic businesses that might arise to serve those farmers and entrepreneurs. It is impossible to lay out all the criteria beforehand for the ECA to follow: Never underestimate the ability of the aid system to hand ordinary business functions to national or international government or NGO agencies instead. Whatever the ECA rules, the aid system will find a way to get around them. Then the ECA will have to adjust the rules.

The ECA's need to adapt to circumstances over time, region by region and country by country, prevents us from deciding on many details of the program far in advance. Ideally, the ECA would have a free hand to set its own rules, but we all know the world as we find it is far from ideal. So the ECA will have to do the best it can with whatever mandate and funding it manages to carve out from the current aid system. The next chapters offer some further details on how to organize the ECA and what roles business, NGOs, government agencies, and ordinary citizens can play in helping it come about and work. The rest of this chapter outlines a plan of action that might set the stage for whatever form the ECA might eventually take in practice.

Our starting point is the successful campaign by the U.S. Committee for Economic Development to explain the Marshall Plan to the American public. For the ECA to even come into existence, we need an equivalent campaign in rich and poor countries alike. At the moment, there is crippling ignorance on both sides about the role of business in fighting poverty. A campaign to explain the need for an ECA can also serve as a mechanism for setting it up.

Here we add a recent trend in "executive education" at business schools, where managers from businesses come together to learn new skills and then plan how to apply them in real projects back at the office. Current and potential aid donors and professionals from countries that receive aid need to learn new skills for promoting domestic business. Foreign and local business schools can use their existing faculty, plus faculty or other experienced professionals from countries that have thriving business sectors or have improved on their *Doing Business* indicators. Each year's *Doing Business* report lists the top ten reformers: Egypt and Colombia are the only countries to repeat on the list for the past two years. So the professionals who had a big hand in making those improvements should teach others what they did. Only then can the "students" join in designing, running, and working with an ECA.

In postwar Europe no one had to explain to Europeans or the Marshall Plan staff the details of how domestic business works. In prewar Europe, business thrived, and there was no competing aid system to confuse everyone about what to do. In poor countries today foreign donors and local professionals alike need to learn how business works and puzzle through how they might promote it locally in the face of great poverty and a competing aid system that will certainly not disappear overnight. In a way this reverses a key sequence in the Marshall Plan, where loans to local business, repaid, funded commercial infrastructure. The ECA has to begin with a key element of commercial infrastructure first: the basic institutions of a thriving business sector. The loans follow.

This brings us back to the ten elements of *Doing Business*. Each country needs a general plan for reforming its ten elements first, then making its ECA loans, and then spending the money repaid on infrastructure. Let's call this the planning phase. Just coming up with the plan will be very costly, because it includes the information and training campaign. Realistically, it must come from grant money, not loans, in order to maintain high standards. If it comes from loan money there is a natural urgency to approve whatever plan arises in order to hurry up and start repaying. This has been one of the fatal flaws of the World Bank's core loan program. Instead, grant funding means you can reject bad plans and move deadlines as needed, to give the planners enough time, flexibility, and money to come up with the best way to undertake business reform in their country.

One key part of this planning phase is an ongoing series of conferences modeled on the industry association meetings that take place every day around the world. Bankers meet to learn the latest about banking. Marketers do the same. Accountants too. Exporters, importers, furniture makers—you name it. There's a national or international meeting on every slice of the business world somewhere, sometime during the year—except in the aid countries. ECA planning needs to fill this gap with similar conferences geared to the slices of business the aid countries need most. Each country's plan will need detail on how to reform different sectors in different ways, and these technical conferences can bring professionals in poor countries up to date on current practice in each sector. But there should be no per diems, a common aid practice, where government officials receive extra pay for participating in development projects.

These conferences also provide a means to attract professionals who fled their homeland for a better life in rich countries. Many would like to return home, if they can make a decent living. The real promise of a future thriving business sector might do it. The conferences lead to more formal planning sessions and the funding of reforms that must precede the ECA loans. For example, a country might need a new cadre of well-paid, well-trained independent judges for commercial courts that include protecting businesses against corrupt demands by police and other government officials. This is complicated, costly, but crucial to do before the loans arrive. In this way, the ECA grants will create quite a few jobs for local professionals early on, and others might return to join businesses to prepare plans to use the loans.

Where will all these grants come from? For that, the ECA needs a second arm or a sister organization—call it the

ECA Foundation—to raise and spend grant funds. In the Anglo-American tradition, an endowed foundation spends only income from its capital and lasts forever. Over recent decades, foundations have generally made a return of 10 percent on their investments, reinvested half of that to keep up with inflation, and spent the remainder—that is, 5 percent. Total aid per year these days is well over $100 billion, so it might be realistic for the ECA Foundation to carve out 1 percent of that over ten years, for a total endowment of $10 billion. That means it would spend $50 million the first year (5 percent × $1 billion) and grow to spend $500 million (5 percent × $10 billion) per year from the tenth year on.

In the first instance, then, a grant-making ECA Foundation would lay the groundwork for the loan-making ECA. Over those ten years we would seek to divert 10 percent of aid per year to the ECA, which would spend its repaid loans on commercial infrastructure and thus disappear over time, after loaning out and then spending a total of $100 billion. The ECA Foundation would have $10 billion left after ten years, enough to give the ECA one more year of life. These are modest targets indeed: diverting a total of 11 percent of aid over ten years for the ECA and the ECA Foundation combined. Perhaps they are too modest. They leave 89 percent of the aid system intact, most of that anti-business. A 50–50 split would be better: charity and business evenly matched, each in its own domain. But 11 percent is at least a good start. An appendix to this book offers a more detailed budget for both the ECA and the ECA Foundation.

To view these numbers in the right light, we need to remember the scale of world poverty. The World Bank reports that 1.4 billion people live on less than $1.25 per day. That's a bit less than $500 per year. To double their income these people need a total of $700 billion per year (1.4 billion × $500). That's about seven times the total world aid budget. If we give the aid as charity and all of it reaches its target—even with absolutely no inefficiency or corruption—then we help them one seventh of the way ($100 billion/$700 billion). Hence the calls to double aid, to help them another one seventh. But even that leaves a gap of five sevenths, or $500 billion per year, forever. Charity can never fill that gap. Even if it did, that still leaves the people poor, living on $1,000 per year. To get them to $2,000 per year, you would need another $1.4 trillion per year, or fourteen times the current annual world aid budget.

You can never deliver enough charity to give poor people a decent life. Business is the only sustainable answer to poverty: It gives people a way to earn money to pay for a decent life themselves. Within rich countries, charity helps the few less fortunate who fall through the cracks of prosperity. It's easy to forget that the business sector creates that prosperity and the charity too, through taxes and private donations. When you extend that charity system to poor countries, it is easy to forget that those countries lack a viable business sector. The answer is not to give more charity—even if you could find $1.4 trillion per year—but to help their business sectors thrive.

Note that a modern Marshall Plan for poor countries gives a big role to government institutions, and the ECA itself would most likely be an NGO of some kind. Pro-business does not mean business-only. And it does not amount to blind faith in free markets. There is no such thing as a completely free market. There never was and never will be. In a free market, buyers and sellers decide what goods they want to exchange, at what price, in contrast to a "controlled" or "regulated" market, where the government influences directly or indirectly what goods are sold and their prices. All markets are regulated to some degree. Some controls are bad, like the government fixing food prices. Some controls are good: Every product sold in rich countries has some kind of health or quality regulation it must conform to somewhere along the line from production to sale.

In general, the move to business from previous systems—tribalism, despotism, feudalism, pure or national socialism—means that markets get freer. But they never end up completely free. If you take the top fifty countries in *Doing Business* 2008—from Singapore, number 1; through Austria, number 25; to Taiwan, number 50—they vary on each of our ten elements to some revealing degree. Their very different historical paths and contemporary circumstances make for very different combinations of rules that govern their markets. And they change to some degree every year. Yet all fifty offer worthy models for the hundred or so aid countries that desperately need to stop suppressing their business sectors. One hundred poor countries, fifty model countries, ten elements—the possible combinations run to the thousands. That's why the ECA cannot possibly lay down a single set of rules for all countries ahead of time. Each country should and will take a different path.

Yet each path will take that particular poor country very far from the aid system it lives under now. That path will not be easy. In most poor countries the current government likes the present system. As the previous chapter showed, there are massive political obstacles to a modern Marshall Plan for poor countries, in rich and poor countries alike. This book is only one step: to make the case and try to win over the hearts and minds of the aid public, the aid profession, and especially the world business sector.

5

CHASE THE DEVIL

Details for a Marshall Model

—

> The older agrarian regimes worked as interlocking systems. It was
> difficult to take an axe to one part without destroying the whole.
>
> —MARC BLOCH, *FRENCH RURAL HISTORY*

The great historian Marc Bloch showed in meticulous detail how difficult it was and how long it took for the old feudal regimes of France to yield to new commercial agriculture. Feudalism had four centuries to take root in France, and over the next four centuries the business system replaced it. That is a warning. There is no quick and easy way for the aid system to yield to a normal pro-business system in the poor countries of the world. The aid system has been with us only five decades, but in that short time its scale and complexity have come to rival the feudal system of Bloch's old France. It will likely take at least four decades for the business system to overtake it.

The previous chapter outlined in broad strokes a decade of funding and spending for an ECA and an ECA Foundation that would apply the business model of the Marshall Plan to poor countries. Both institutions would likely need to continue in some form for at least another three decades. They would adjust over time to changing circumstances, along with the world economy and the poor countries themselves. This chapter offers some possible details on how to structure the first decade. In particular, we look to integrate elements from recent or current programs, especially those that already target the business sector in poor countries. As with our look back to the original Marshall Plan, there is no need to reinvent the wheel. We can pick out what we need in the future from the vast storehouse of the past.

The devil is in the details, and here we dive into them. The result is a list of many actions, some large and some small, for the future ECA and ECA Foundation to undertake. They might seem piecemeal, and that's right. The result is not a single coordinated plan, a giant clockwork with the pieces all moving in synch, but rather an umbrella for many different parts moving in many different directions at many different times in many different places, to make a complex, diverse ecosystem. That's how business works, and how the original Marshall Plan succeeded.

THE MARSHALL PLAN IN GREECE

We can best understand how to adapt the key technical details of the Marshall Plan by taking the case of Greece. In its economy and politics, Greece was the Marshall

Plan country most like poor countries today from various angles: in population, economy, and politics. The example of Greece gives us both concrete ideas to borrow and the hope it can work again.

Greece is smaller than the major countries of Europe. Its population at the time was 7.5 million, versus nearly 50 million each for Britain, France, Germany, and Italy. Of the sixteen Marshall Plan countries, Greece was the third poorest and the most unstable at the time. Only Portugal and Turkey were poorer, but both escaped most of the fighting of World War II. Greece suffered invasion from both Italy and Germany, which an active Greek resistance fought with the help of the British army. After the war the resistance split and fought a civil war: Greek communists with Russian help versus Greek royalists and democrats with British help. So among the war-torn countries, Greece was the poorest and stayed war-torn longest. And it was less than a full democracy before, during, and right after the Marshall Plan: The Greek king stayed in power to some degree through the 1940s and 1950s.

Small, poor, war-torn, and semi-democratic—that sounds a lot like many poor countries today, especially in Africa. Of course, Greece did not have forty years of aid to undo. And although its farmland was the poorest in Europe, it still had its ancient advantages of a single written language, excellent ports, and a prime location at the hub of Mediterranean trade. We cannot expect most poor countries to mimic Greece's success in whole. But how the

Marshall Plan helped, at scale and quickly, is worth learn-
ing from and mimicking in part.

The original Marshall Plan spent a different amount per
person in all its sixteen countries, and the new one would do
the same. Three percent of Marshall funds went to Greece:
$366 million out of $12.7 billion total. That's about $50 per
person for Greece, or $400 adjusted to today. By compari-
son, in the last chapter we estimated a ten-year budget of
about $100 billion for the ECA and ECA Foundation com-
bined, over ten years: divided by the 1.5 billion poor people
in the poor countries of the world. This would make $67
per person, or about one sixth of what the Marshall Plan
spent in Greece. If only half the poor countries joined in,
that amount would double. And if the ECA had twice the
funds we estimated, that amount would double again.

In one sense the Marshall Plan began with Greece. In
postwar Europe, communism threatened to spread west in
many countries, but especially France and Greece. In France
the Communist Party might win an election. In Greece the
communist fighters might take Athens. In February 1947
came crisis: Britain's lack of funds for its own recovery led
it to cut off military aid to Greece. The Americans rushed
in, first with direct military aid and then, thanks to General
George C. Marshall, a recovery plan for not just Greece but
all of western Europe.

A month before the Greek crisis, in January 1947, President Truman named Marshall his secretary of state. A month
after the Greek crisis, in March, the president announced

American military aid to Greece. In April, Marshall met with the foreign ministers of Europe in Moscow to arrive at a final treaty for Germany and Austria. There he saw firsthand how the Soviet Union wanted to continue expanding into the West, and how the economic collapse of the West was helping. Marshall asked George Kennan of the Foreign Service to put together a working group and propose a program of economic aid to Europe. Kennan delivered his report on May 23. Four days later, a second report came from Marshall's undersecretary of state for economic affairs, William Clayton, a former business executive from the cotton industry. Marshall discussed both reports with his staff and advisors. A week later, on June 5, Marshall announced his plan in a speech at Harvard's commencement.

Here in part are his words:

The breakdown of the business structure of Europe during the war was complete.... The restoration or maintenance in European countries of principles of individual liberty, free institutions, and genuine independence rests largely upon the establishment of sound economic conditions, stable international economic relationships, and the achievement of the countries of Europe of a healthy economy independent of extraordinary outside assistance. The accomplishment of these objectives calls for a plan of European recovery, open to all such nations which cooperate in such a plan, based upon a strong production effort, the expansion of foreign trade, the creation and maintenance of internal financial stability, and the development of economic cooperation, including all possible steps to establish and maintain equitable rates of exchange and to bring about the progressive elimination of trade barriers.

Marshall does not exactly list the ten elements of *Doing Business*, but he gives a good start. From Kennan's and Clayton's report, through Marshall's speech, and on to the detailed planning of that summer and fall, the details of how to support the business sector of western Europe became clear. From first to last, the Marshall Plan aimed at business, not charity. Many aid agencies were already working in Europe, especially the United Nations Relief and Rehabilitation Administration from 1943 to 1947, which handed over to the International Relief Organization in 1948. In postwar Europe, then, business support followed refugee relief. Contrast that with the recent decades in poor countries, where NGOs entered for disaster relief and then followed that with charitable village projects, not business.

There was nothing in Marshall's personal background to make him especially pro-business. His father owned his own company, selling coal in Pennsylvania, but the son never worked for it. The company suffered in the recession of 1893, so it did not appear to offer an immediate future for the boy. In 1897, at the age of seventeen, George enrolled in a state college, the Virginia Military Institute. He graduated in 1901, and joined the army. From there he worked his way up through the ranks, to become a key staff planner for American troops in World War I and then a general in 1936. Three years later President Roosevelt made him army chief of staff. That made him America's most important military commander during World War II. He never fought directly in that war: Eisenhower, in Europe, and MacArthur, in the Pacific, reported to Marshall in Washington.

At no time during those army years did Marshall have any more contact or show any greater interest in business than other American officers. Truman appointed him Secretary of State because he was a good diplomat and planner, not for any pro-business stance. And Truman himself was a Democrat. The Republicans were the more pro-business party. Marshall's speech, and the plan that followed, sprang not from any unusual knowledge or commitment to business but from the ordinary, mainstream American mentality that business was the source of mass prosperity. To this day the two main American political parties still agree on that, and probably always will.

Soon after his speech, Marshall invited all countries of Europe, including the Soviet Union, to meet in Paris from July 12th on to begin working out the details. The Soviets and the nations of Eastern Europe declined, although Czechoslovakia accepted at first and others, such as Hungary, would have attended if the Soviets had let them. Clayton led the American delegation. On July 21, Kennan reported to Marshall by memo the results of the Paris convention: "We have no plan." Instead the Europeans proposed various structures, programs, and amounts for the plan overall and for each country. There was little agreement. Yet Marshall was pleased. The Europeans had the first go at the details. He wanted them to design their own program as much as possible. The Paris conference never really ended. It broke up gradually into work and reports by committees, with Marshall's staff alongside. The final report came out in September.

Right away we see an element to carry forward to our new ECA. The government of each poor country must agree to the ECA operating there. So a first step for the ECA is to invite poor countries to a meeting like the Paris conference of July 1947. Those who decline miss their chance to join and to influence the outcome. Over the following months the country delegates and ECA staff work together to hammer out the details of how the program will work.

But we expect some differences too. The European delegates in July 1947 all understood the business sector. That's not the case for many poor countries today. The ECA will have to negotiate with each country the composition of their delegation, to include the legitimate business sector. Those businesses will likely include domestic and foreign firms. And the Marshall Plan had a single sponsor: The ECA will likely have many sponsors. So those sponsors will need to hammer out their own structure during the conference too. It will all be very complicated. But the Marshall Plan points the way.

Three kinds of committees came out of the Paris conference. First, a Committee of European Economic Co-operation (CEEC) included all the participating European countries as members. Our new ECA might do the same, either worldwide or by region, such as Latin America and the Caribbean, Africa, the Middle East, and Asia. Europe, after all, is a region. Next, an Executive Committee of five countries convened the CEEC and oversaw the Technical Committees that did the detailed work from July to September. Marshall and his staff chose the five. For various political reasons specific to the time and place, they were Britain, France, Italy, the Netherlands, and Norway. Some other countries objected, of course. Our new ECA would need an equivalent Executive Committee, likewise chosen by the ECA itself. And the Technical Committees would carry over completely to the new ECA.

The Executive and Technical committees dissolved in September. Their role was to help design the plan, not implement it. The CEEC became the permanent Organization for European Economic Co-operation (OEEC), to continue as the regional coordinating body for the plan. From October to March American advocates of the Marshall Plan sold it to their public and Congress. The Committee for Economic Development (CED), founded in 1942, played a key role. It was a group of business leaders who spun off from the Commerce Department's Business Advisory Council to work with government departments as the voice of the private sector in wartime economic policy. The first president of the CED was Paul Hoffman, head of the car maker Studebaker. The U.S. Congress passed the Marshall Plan in March 1948. The ECA came into existence, replacing the Paris Executive Committee and Marshall's own planning staff. President Truman named Hoffman head of the ECA.

We are a long way from Greece, but all these details matter for how the Marshall Plan worked there. Greece took part in every step on the European side. The program began in April 1948. At that point Greece had a one-year plan for items it needed to buy and what it wanted to do with the money Greek businesses repaid. Marshall's staff approved the plan. For future years Hoffman's ECA staff took over. Each year Greece submitted a new one-year plan. This same one-year routine can carry over to the new ECA.

We turn now to how the Marshall Plan worked for Greece. The one-year Greek plan included contracting details and delivery dates. The ECA released that to U.S. businesses through the normal channels of the export-import trade: the U.S. Department of Commerce, press releases, and industry journals. A U.S. business contacted the Greek business directly. The ECA made sure that normal market prices prevailed, and issued a letter of commitment to a U.S. bank, which in turn arranged letters of credit with the Greek bank of the Greek business. The U.S. bank made a loan to the Greek business by paying the bill to the Greek bank. The ECA then reimbursed the U.S. bank in dollars, out of a revolving fund for Greece at the U.S. Treasury. The amount of the total fund and of its annual use made up part of the annual Greek plan that the ECA approved.

In Greece the farmer or factory paid the Greek bank in drachmas, usually in installments as a loan. Instead of paying the U.S. bank in turn, the Greek bank forwarded the money to a Greek Treasury counterpart fund. The Greek government then used 95 percent of those funds for projects within Greece, as approved by the ECA in the annual plan. The other 5 percent went to the ECA for administrative costs.

There were other payment mechanisms too. Greece could pay with dollars from its own foreign exchange, for later reimbursement by the ECA; or issue an ECA draft through the U.S. Federal Reserve in favor of U.S. suppliers; or ask the ECA to issue a letter of commitment to the supplier, pledging direct payment without a bank. These alternative mechanisms were mostly for large shipments of commodities such as grain, oil, or steel, for very large Greek businesses.

The new ECA needs to adopt the same kind of flexible financing as the old ECA. The essential idea is the same: to turn aid into effective support for the entire domestic business sector in poor countries. Many elements can carry over intact, for example, the revolving fund by country. U.S. banks advancing payment for U.S. products will likely not be needed, because today all countries have easy access to world trade and various forms of financing for whatever they need to buy. All funding will be grants or loans to local firms and organizations, not ECA contracts that those entities implement. Contrast that with the typical aid project, where the local organization is a sub-contractor who hands over receipts payment-by-payment for a project that the aid agency manages. Under the ECA, businesses and other organizations manage directly and report income and expenses by normal business accounting procedures.

Over the four years of the Marshall Plan, Greece spent less than half of its counterpart funds (45 percent), thus leaving a healthy balance for the future. Like most other war-torn Marshall Plan countries, what Greece did spend went first for physical reconstruction: housing, public buildings, roads, railroads, and ports (31 percent). Unlike other Marshall Plan countries, because of its ongoing civil war, Greece spent a good share of its counterpart funds on refugee relief (29 percent). As a poor country, it also spent a good share on agriculture (13 percent), especially land reclamation, the purchase of livestock, and a research and extension system. And it made further loans to private Greek businesses of all kinds (7 percent). Next came sanitation and public health (3 percent), including a malaria campaign.

This spending pattern of counterpart funds shows that most of the money helped business: agricultural and commercial infrastructure, including a direct re-lending program for businesses. Not only did the Marshall Plan turn aid into effective financing for the whole Greek business sector, but it made Greek public spending dependent on the volume of business. If Greek business thrived, it bought more inputs and paid more money into the government counterpart fund. That fund in turn spent most of the money to support more business. All these elements carry over intact to the new ECA.

The Marshall Plan included a technical assistance program, separate from the country programs, where American experts advised European businesses and government agencies and Europeans traveled to the U.S. to study American businesses. The whole program took up only 1.5 percent of the total Marshall Plan budget. Greeks participated, and asked for even more. The civil war lasted until 1949, and even after that instability continued. In 1950 alone, there were five different governments. This wreaked havoc on Marshall Plan administration, as government agency staff came and went. Many Greeks asked the Americans to take over the Greek side of administering the Plan, but they refused. That was the right response, so Greeks worked out the institutional arrangements that must endure after the Marshall money was gone.

Contrast that with the many foreigners that aid agencies post to design and run government and NGO projects in poor countries, to make sure the project goes right. But it goes right only as long as the foreigners remain, and then it falls apart. That's project assistance, not technical assistance. The difference between the two is crucial. In project assistance, the foreigners manage the project. In technical assistance, the local company or organization runs the project, and technical assistants advise them on aspects of the project where they have special expertise. Decades ago in aid to poor countries, technical assistance was the norm. Mismanagement by the local entity led aid agencies gradually to shift to project assistance, though they still call it technical assistance. Like the original, the new ECA should fund technical assistance, not project assistance. If the local entity fails, it goes out of business, instead of getting propped up forever by foreigners who run the show.

Because the Greek government was in such bad shape, a share of its counterpart spending (3 percent) went to a special technical assistance program to reduce and reform it. In most poor countries aid has funded many technical assistance programs to reform government agencies, but without an internal financing mechanism like the counterpart fund or an overall reorientation toward business like the Marshall Plan. Although the scale of institutional disorder in most poor countries means that the ECA Foundation will have to spend grant money on institutional reform, including a portion in ECA financing is a good discipline to carry over from the original.

Contrast the Marshall Plan's tight financing formula with the World Bank's standard practice. In the Marshall Plan, businesses repaid loans and advances, and that money funded government projects directly. In poor countries today the World Bank staff designs projects for the government to implement and then calculates how much that will boost the overall economy. It adds up the projects to arrive at a total projected economic increase and then calculates the extra taxes the government will collect. It then gives a huge loan for the government to pay back with the future taxes from the future economic growth. Five years later, when the growth has not happened and the government can't pay back the loan, the bank rolls it over or aid activists campaign for the bank to forgive it. Meanwhile, the bank has designed another set of projects that are already under way, with another loan the government will never repay.

The Marshall Plan encountered more obstacles in Greece than in other countries, but still the program worked. The Greek economy grew 30 percent over the four years of the plan and then took off in the 1950s, when Greece grew faster than any other country in the world except for Japan. But the ECA faced problems not only in Greece and the other Marshall Plan countries but in Washington too. There Hoffman fought off two sets of fellow Americans: officials from other agencies and industry lobbies.

Many State Department officials wanted the ECA under them, because it dealt with foreign affairs, but Marshall wisely decided to make it independent. Even so, officials in the State, Treasury, Commerce, and Agriculture departments wanted the ECA to hire staff from them and to work through them when it stepped on their turf, which was all the time. Instead Hoffman staffed the ECA in Washington mostly with fellow business executives, corporate lawyers, and investment bankers, and he tried his best to run the Marshall Plan on straight business principles rather than according to the policies of the various departments. He won all major battles, although the struggles continued throughout the four years of the plan.

The industry lobbies were another matter. Hoffman wanted American business to compete on an equal basis with foreign business for Marshall Plan contracts. But the U.S. shipping lobby managed to write into the Marshall Plan law that 50 percent of all commodities under the Plan travel in U.S. ships. The wheat industry got in too, at 25 percent. The aluminum industry tried for 50 percent, but Hoffman was able to kill that in Congress. He then judged that U.S. shippers were overcharging, so he threatened to ignore the 50 percent rule. The shipping lobby fought back with a public relations campaign. So Hoffman threatened to quit. In the end he lost that round and stayed on. Later he managed to kill the wheat rule.

The new ECA has much to learn from Hoffman's struggles with competing agencies and industry lobbies. Donors to the new ECA must give it the same bureaucratic autonomy that Marshall gave the original. The same nationalistic procurement rules that Hoffman fought against still bedevil foreign aid today, not just for commodities like food aid but for technical—and project—assistance, where American agencies hire American companies and the British do the same for the French. The Danish will want a certain technical institute they fund at home to run some technical project in Guatemala. The French will insist on a certain percentage of French citizens on the ECA staff. The Americans will try to re-create the U.S. land-grant university system in every country. And so on around the donor table. This is common aid practice, and for the ECA it will have to stop. That will be very hard to achieve. Each donor will want the ECA to promote its own policies, people, and institutions in the same way the American departments wanted Hoffman to promote theirs.

Last but not least, we must recognize the Marshall Plan's effect on European economic integration. There is no direct link: The European Union began as a regional coal agreement in 1951, then became a European Economic Community in 1957. But the indirect link is strong. The ECA forced the countries to come together on a single plan in Paris over the summer and fall of 1947, and they did. The ECA also forced them to open their borders to each other. And they did. The ECA's regional body, the OEEC, was too much an American creation, so the Europeans set up their own. All the poor regions of the world feature countries that are too small to thrive on their own, and most of them pay lip-service to regional integration, but the real problem is how. The new ECA can help, just like the original in Europe.

From Washington to Greece these myriad details start to point the way for how the new ECA might work. Many details will differ: For example, there won't be tractors and flour from America. But the structure and mechanisms of the old and new will be essentially the same—the same software, different hardware, for a different time and a different place. In that way the Marshall Plan remains timeless and universal, and the best hope to fight poverty in the poor countries of the world.

BUSINESS CLIMATE INITIATIVES

The original Marshall Plan gives us an overall design for our new ECA. To fill in more of the details, we find in Latin America a recent example of a funding agency using a version of the *Doing Business* elements to help countries reform. In 1959 the Organization of American States created the Inter-American Development Bank (IDB), which currently makes loans and grants of $10 billion per year to twenty-six countries in the region. Its program overall has been typical of the usual aid system. Starting in 2003, though, it began a Business Climate Initiative (BCI) to promote local business. But big aid agencies reorganize often, and the BCI vanished sometime in 2006, when it published its last annual report for 2005. But that's not the BCI's fault. It still offers a good model to draw from for how the ECA might structure its own core program.

The BCI went in three steps. First, it signed a voluntary Aide-Mémoire—memorandum of understanding—with a government in the region. That showed that the government was interested in business reform and agreed to a specific timetable for the next two steps. Over its short life it managed to sign such memoranda with twenty-four out of its twenty-six active countries. Second, the BCI sent in a diagnostic team to work with the national government and business sector to design jointly a reform program for the country. The 2005 report tells us that "most countries" completed this step. The third step was financing:

Once identified in the country strategies, the specific action plans will be supported through the IDB's operational programs. To this end, the Bank will deploy all its relevant instruments, including policy-based lending, investment loans, technical assistance, and engagement in strategic partnerships.

Therein lies the rub: The BCI depended on the rest of the IDB to fund and carry out the results of the first two steps. The 2005 report tells us that, "Eighteen projects that have BCI components were approved during the year, for an amount of $9.25 million." That's a paltry amount, and they weren't even fully BCI projects. No wonder the BCI faded away. The funding and operational arms of the IDB could simply ignore it. The BCI did not have the authority to take that crucial third step. But the ECA would have that authority. That would allow the ECA to move on to complete the three steps that the BCI laid out but was never able to do. The result would be a comprehensive set of fully funded activities to reform the local business environment.

Africa has a weaker version of the BCI, an Investment Climate Facility (ICF). The name alone tells us that it's not quite on track: It announces that Africa's biggest problem is attracting investment. That's not quite right: The biggest problem is the overall business environment, which includes the investment climate. Remember that many poor countries make it easy for a foreign company to invest in operations locally but keep it hard for local businesses to operate. Total investment can go up, while the local business sector stays down.

In any event, the ICF is the only pan-African agency dedicated exclusively to improving some part of the business climate in Africa. That's a good thing. It started out as an idea from the British government, which brought in the World Bank and other smaller funders (for example, Unilever put in $1 million). So far it has raised about $100 million. As of October 2008 it had ten projects in ten countries, such as reforming the value-added tax in Lesotho and customs systems in Senegal. It does not attempt the kind of comprehensive reform that the BCI aimed for. But it's a good start, and it might even be a candidate for turning into the ECA, if it takes up the BCI method and gains the funding and authority that the regional development banks like the IDB enjoy.

The other two major regional development banks have no major business climate projects. The Asian Development Bank lists "private sector development" as one of eight items in its poverty reduction framework. As usual, the other seven elements undermine the business sector. It's a similar story at the African Development Bank. We see "Private Sector" on its list of topics, but again there are seven other topics on the list that reinforce government rather than business development. It's had a Private Sector window since 1991, but no special activities to improve the business climate in African countries. That was one reason the ICF set itself up as a separate entity.

Among the bilateral aid agencies, USAID has increased

its business support recently, but again alongside much larger conventional programs that undermine business at the same time. Economic Growth and Trade is one of its nine major areas, and within that seven out of thirteen subtopics are conventional. But the other six are good: Enterprise Development, Legal and Institutional Reform, Microenterprise, Privatization, Financial Markets, and Development Credit. Not all of even these are fully for business. Overall we might estimate that only 10 percent of USAID supports local business. Still, that's a vast improvement over past decades. And there is much the ECA can learn and possibly mimic in part from what USAID has done.

The United Kingdom's Department for International Development (DFID) has gone the other way: It makes direct deposits into the accounts of the government in the countries it aids. Ironically, DFID also has one of the most sophisticated business support units among the major donors, called the Growth and Investment Group. It has developed some excellent small projects, such as Challenge Funds. There are a number of such competitive funding mechanisms that the ECA can learn from: USAID's Sustainable Financing Initiative in the 1990s reviewed best practices of many others, and these are well worth the ECA studying. An NGO example is the African Enterprise Challenge Fund (AECF), a creation of the Rockefeller and Gates foundations, funded by five multilateral and bilateral agencies such as the African Development Bank and the British and Dutch official aid agencies.

The AECF currently has funding for $7.5 million per year in grants or subsidized loans, through proposal competitions, to the business sector to support agriculture in sub-Saharan Africa. Based in Kenya, the AECF seems to have a solid mix of local and international business organizations running it: KPMG Development Services Limited, Triple Line Consulting, Imani Development Group, Crown Agents, the Springfield Centre for Business in Development, and Y&R Brands. Yet this infrastructure is quite cumbersome for such a tiny project: two foundations, five funders, and six managing companies. It seems like another bloated development project, rather than a lean entrepreneurial initiative. But the basic model is useful to learn from: a locally based entity that supports business with funding and support from a range of specialized agencies.

The Gates and Howard Buffett foundations have recently started another project that means well but unfortunately sets back the private sector in Africa. The U.N.'s World Food Programme typically buys food for food aid from rich countries, but this new project will collect grain from private African farms instead. That's the good news. The bad news is that it's another case of the "allanblackia problem" we encountered earlier: Instead of businesses serving the private farmers, World Food Programme staff do it. This impedes the normal development of a business sector in food markets. It allows the governments to give farmers some income and get cheap food to their people while still preserving their anti-business policies.

A few other private-sector support projects are worth studying, such as Canada's Financial Sector Reform and Strengthening Initiative, the Private Infrastructure Development Group, and the Commonwealth Business Group. All are small but offer some good element for the ECA to learn from or work with on the ground. Anyone trying to support the business sector in poor countries is a potential ally for the ECA, because the aid industry as a whole continues on its merry way with business an afterthought or forgotten completely.

For example, the major agencies met for the third time in Ghana in September 2008 in a High-Level Forum on Aid Effectiveness. They listed all kinds of problems in the aid system they want to fix, such as too many foreign consultants and not enough donor collaboration on the ground. They did not mention the business sector at all. And *The Economist* reported on the meeting with a favorable full-page article that failed to mention business either—and that from the leading magazine of classical liberalism in the world. Those few hardy souls who have struggled to support the local business sector in the current aid system still face an uphill battle against overwhelming forces: But the ECA can help, and possibly turn the tide.

IS IT CULTURE?

The original Marshall Plan gives us an overall structure, and more recent aid projects give us many elements to borrow from, but actual progress on the ground depends on whether the local people can move from their current systems to the new business system the ECA promotes. There is a widespread notion in many poor countries that business cannot work there because it runs counter to their ancient culture. President Nyerere of Tanzania said exactly that in his Arusha Declaration of 1967. Is it true? If so, the ECA cannot work.

Let's hear from the Ghanaian economist George Ayittey for guidance. In his 2005 book *Africa Unchained*, Ayittey shows that traditional African culture was not at all anti-business. He gives a blow-by-blow account of how postcolonial African governments, with the help of foreign aid, stifled the African business sector. For example, he cites this testimony from an economic advisor of Kwame Nkrumah, first president of Ghana, after ten years of Nkrumah's rule:

It has been the system to gradually stifle the big businessmen and the small Ghanaian businessman in this country to be replaced by State Corporations, and there has been a move towards this in putting all sorts of inconveniences in the way of merchants and traders in the country. The steps to be taken against them were income tax, various types of taxation, license restrictions; African businessmen must not be given licenses and if they persisted they should be given such licenses as would make them incapable of doing business.

EMMANUEL AYEH-KUMI, TESTIMONY TO THE OLLENNU COMMISSION, 1967

At the time of independence in 1956, Ghana had a thriving domestic business sector that benefited from doing business with larger foreign firms, mostly British. By the time of the Ollennu Commission a decade later, after a coup deposed Nkrumah, business in Ghana was stunted and corrupted. The official title of the Ollennu Commission was "Commission of Enquiry into Irregularities and Malpractices in the Grant of Import Licenses." The many restrictions on local business gave government officials in charge of issuing them a vast market for corruption: If you wanted one of the few licenses, you had to pay a bribe to get it. N. A. Ollennu, a distinguished lawyer and head of the commission, summarized his findings as follows: Except for licenses to government departments and state enterprises and licenses "granted upon personal contacts made with the Minister... all others had to pay a bribe between 5 per cent and 10 per cent of the value of the license to be granted."

For example, Okai, a weaver in Kumasi, applied to import yarn. Two of his customers, Akyeampong and Mac Bruce, went to the Ministry of Trade and came back to tell Okai that "the Minister had asked for a £5,000 commission in order to issue him with a £50,000 license." Okai could not afford that, so he offered £3,000. No deal. In another case the minister of trade, A. Y. K. Djin, set up a company and proceeded to grant himself import licenses: "This gave Djin great financial advantage as other firms were not getting licenses.... I find that Djin's action in this regard is a gross abuse of public office."

Here is how Ollennu ends his summary report:

> My greatest hope and my most humble and fervent prayers are that our Ghanaian society, and particularly our youth, should be admonished and inspired by the outcome of this Commission to aspire to honesty and diligence, to the attainment and maintenance of that social and economic order of society in which a man's ambition is to live by the sweat of his face, and so eat the labour of his hands, the blessed heritage of the man that fears the Lord, and works in His ways.

Unfortunately, the next governments of Ghana ignored the Ollennu Commission and things got even worse. Bribes of only 5 to 10 percent of gross seem quaint today, although as a share of Okai's profits it was closer to 50 percent. But Ayittey and many other courageous Africans keep the spirit of Ollennu alive. Ayittey gives a crisp summary of how Africa went astray in the early years of independence:

> Socialism was by far the most predominant ideology adopted by African nationalist leaders. The hegemonic

role in economic development envisaged for the state was driven by this ideology since many African nationalist leaders were suspicious of capitalism. The courtship and fascination with socialism emerged during the struggle for political independence and freedom from colonial rule in the 1950s. Many African nationalists harbored a deep distrust and distaste for capitalism, which was falsely identified by most African nationalist leaders as an extension of colonialism and imperialism. Therefore, freedom from colonial rule was synonymous with freedom from capitalism. This spawned the belief among African leaders that the most appropriate strategy by which they could undertake national development was socialism. Furthermore, having just emerged from the colonial era, all African leaders were naturally poised to jealously guard against another episode of "colonial" and foreign exploitation. This was only possible if the state maintained a large enough presence in the economy, ostensibly to control the activities of foreign companies.

Ayittey goes on to quote Jennifer Whitaker of the U.S. Council on Foreign Relations on the role of foreign aid after independence:

Like the World Bank, the United States saw the development process in those days the way most Africans did: governments would expand and diversify the economy by creating industries and services, moving into areas where Europeans and Asians sometimes held a near monopoly.... Ghana proved an apt student of this new science, pioneering the multi-year comprehensive development plans.... The plans grew increasingly sophisticated as economists invented new techniques, including input-output analysis, growth simulation models, and dynamic programming. Development programs, national planning boards, and industrial development corporations sprang up everywhere.

Ayittey surveys the mix of disastrous government and aid policies that left Africa in such a mess by the twenty-first century. He tells us an African Union report of August 2004 calculated that "Africa loses an estimated $148 billion annually to corrupt practices, a figure which represents 25 percent of the continent's Gross Domestic Product." Ayittey blames directly the system of state development and the system of foreign aid for funding this corrupt system. He calls both systems counter to the indigenous African economic system, which he calls a "Free Market, Free Trade Tradition."

For Ayittey the period from 1880 to 1950 was the "golden age of peasant prosperity in Africa." Like tribal societies elsewhere in the world, from ancient Mesopotamia to the present day, once trade opened up with the outside world the indigenous farmers and artisans made and sold whatever they could for the market. Ayittey tells us, "The fundamental point is that African natives had the *economic freedom* to decide for themselves what crops they could cultivate—cash crops or food crops—and what to do with the proceeds." Starting with Ghana in the 1950s and then in other African countries as they gained independence, the state and aid systems took over instead, in the same way that feudalism, despotism, pure and national socialism took over from tribal economies elsewhere in the world.

Ayittey's book is a call to action to the younger generation of Africans, in the spirit of N. A. Olennu's plaintive cry nearly forty years before. Ayittey calls past African leaders the "hippo" generation: "stodgy, pudgy, and wedded to the old colonialism/imperialism paradigm with an abiding faith in the potency of the state." But for Ayittey:

Wealth is created in the private sector, not in the government sector. Therefore, those African elites who want to get wealthy—and there is nothing wrong with wanting to be rich—should seek their own place in the private sector, even if they have to produce and sell donkey carts. And there is nothing wrong with becoming rich by producing donkey carts or services the poor want.

Ayittey looks to the young of Africa as the "cheetah" generation: "They tend to be young African graduates, who are dynamic, intellectually agile, and pragmatic.... Their minds are not polluted with all this anticolonial rhetoric and garbage." He cites as an example the Ghana Investment

Club, a "pack of cheetahs who mobilized young Ghanaian professionals in the diaspora ... to mobilize funds for investment in Ghana. They were not waiting for the World Bank to do it for them." Another example is the Kenyan Students for Free Enterprise, "a group of young university students that are involved in community-based entrepreneurship projects in the Marurui and Kibera slums of Nairobi."

Ayittey's ultimate aim is "unleashing the entrepreneurial talents and creative energies of the real African people." So too the ECA. Ayittey's cheetahs will be the first to benefit. And through them, all of Africa.

FOREIGN BUSINESS

In the previous section we saw how postcolonial African governments stifled both the foreign and local business sectors. Yet is that half right? Perhaps the answer is to support local business but stifle foreign business. After all, many poor countries justify their restrictions on the business sector as a way to prevent foreign businesses from taking over. And they are half right. An open door has always meant that firms from countries with more advanced business sectors will outdo local firms at first. The leading historical example is England. The industrial revolution began there, so England preached free trade around the world, and sometimes sent in its gunboats to force it. Most countries threw up some kind of barrier to protect their domestic firms against English ones, including the United States.

In the same way, foreign firms dominated the local business sector in most poor countries during the colonial era. Later, most of the new governments squeezed them out. Sometimes they used force: Uganda's military dictator, Idi Amin, threw the Indian traders out of the country, to great popular acclaim. Many Malays resented Chinese business success, which ended up in Singapore and Malaysia splitting into two separate countries. In South Africa restrictions against African business are gone, but white South Africans had such a head start they remain far in the lead. How much to squeeze white business remains a heated debate within the ruling African National Congress.

The long-term answer is simple: Foreign businesses are the best teachers for domestic business. The domestic business sectors of Singapore, Ireland, India, and the United States all served as apprentices to English firms. In chapter 4, we saw the modern example of Daewoo in Bangladesh. China's apprenticeship is vast and explicit. But all that's long-term, and as Keynes famously remarked, in the long run we're all dead. In the here and now the ECA will have to favor domestic firms over foreign, for political ease and because of its mission to hasten the growth of the domestic business sector.

There is a wide body of good and bad practice in affirmative action for local firms around the world. The ECA will learn from these precedents. But nowhere is it easy to do.

There are countless tricks to make a foreign firm look domestic. For example, you hire a local citizen to register a local company and receive a modest salary as the CEO, and then you operate the whole thing as a foreign company. The government responds with rules that force you to hire local employees. So you hire a few, but mostly you use your own foreign staff. So the government limits your hiring to only those posts you can't find local citizens for. That means you submit a form for every new person you want to hire, for a government official to review and approve. Eventually we are back to a whole host of restrictions, and a low score on *Doing Business*.

In the end, if the ECA works well, there is no way to avoid an increase in foreign business in poor countries. Thirty years after Idi Amin, the Indian traders are returning to Uganda, and the local people this time are happy to see them. Where African countries have shut down their corrupt cotton-marketing boards, foreign cotton companies are returning to the countryside to fill the gap, again with the thanks of African farmers. A French firm, Bolloré, has taken over many port logistics and now handles most of Africa's cocoa, coffee, cotton, rubber, and timber.

Yet foreign business alone cannot rescue poor countries. Various commodity booms—especially in oil—have given some poor countries good overall growth rates over the past decade, and an increase in foreign investment often accompanied those booms. But that is an old story—it has happened periodically over the past forty years. And once again, local policies that block the local business sector have prevented it from taking part in the growth or investment. So the ultimate solution to poverty in those countries remains beyond reach. In a similar vein Dambisa Moyo argues in Dead Aid for African governments to reject aid and raise bonds in the international capital market instead. Moyo is right in her critique of past aid, but unfortunately her prescription does not address the local government's suppression of local business: instead it gives governments an alternative way to raise money for the same old government development projects.

Over the past decade, more and more of the foreign businesses that operate in poor countries have been Chinese. In Africa, for example, Chinese firms have helped China rise to second place after the United States among the continent's trading partners—ahead of even Britain and France, the former colonial powers. Chinese companies often arrive with some kind of subsidy from the Chinese government, including grants and loans to the local government. Otherwise they mostly operate like other foreign firms, with little impact on the local business sector, except that they hire less local labor and bring over Chinese instead. In a country low on the Doing Business list, it doesn't matter if the foreign firms are Chinese, British, Japanese, French, or American: Local business can't do business with them.

If a country is high on the *Doing Business* list, foreign companies can operate normally. That makes it easy for the ECA to identify domestic firms for help. If a country is low on the list, there is more incentive for tricks that hide foreign firms as domestic, or for a government to permit foreign business and collect big fees from it rather than allow local firms to thrive. In that case the ECA will have a harder time sorting out which firms to support before the reforms kick in, and might need alternative mechanisms for a while, such as financing contracts between foreign and local firms rather than directing loans to the local firm itself.

Race, of course, makes it all much harder. The Irish, once victims of England, achieved prosperity in the end by adopting the British business system. But both peoples were white. Apprenticeship is much harder when the apprentice is a black African or a Quechua Indian and the teacher is white, in a country where colonial rule and racial discrimination went hand in hand. The ECA must take this too into account, especially where it has a say in local staffing. But note: Working for a big foreign company is today one of the best paths to success for a former victim of racial discrimination. And professionals from the vast diaspora who have fled poor countries over the past few decades can use a job at foreign firms in their home countries as a steppingstone back to the local business sector. Global firms are modern leaders in staff diversity, not through the goodness of their hearts but because in this day and age, in this complex world, it's good business to take in ideas from everywhere.

In a normal country foreign business is good for local business. The ECA will favor local business, but not against foreign business. The main battle is elsewhere: local business versus the abnormal economic activity of state agencies and NGOs. In that struggle local and foreign business are allies.

DOING BUSINESS

Throughout this book we look to the World Bank's *Doing Business* indicators as our key elements that make local business thrive, and as the main measures the new Marshall Plan will use to guide its policies. Yet the ECA must take them with a very large dose of salt. As scientific measurements, they are very far from perfect. At best they offer a generic list of measures a country can undertake, and a rough scale of which countries are farthest along that path. Some countries, like Georgia and Mauritius, have taken the *Doing Business* list and aimed explicitly to rise higher in the rankings. In some cases, though, the indicators do not give a good picture of the domestic business sector. We take these anomalies as a warning: The ECA can use the list for a first look at any particular country but then must dig deeper to understand each country on its own.

For example, India ranked 120th out of 178 countries in 2008. It came out well in only two indicators: getting credit (36th) and protecting investors (33rd). Reforms on these two measures alone have let local Indian companies spring up and operate somewhat normally at small, medium, and large scale. And India's pure and national socialism put it so far behind that placing 120th is a sign of real progress. Also, India has an educated population, a strong heritage of the British business system, and fertile temperate farmland, so small reforms can have a big impact. But ranking 120th still means that India has a long way to go if it wants to bring the rest of its vast population out of poverty.

Another anomaly is Greece. It ranked 100th in 2008, with high scores only in dealing with licenses (42nd) and closing a business (38th). Many state industries operate alongside normal domestic and foreign businesses, corruption is rife, and still Greece thrives. There are three reasons for this. First, Greece still profits from its historic location at the hub of Mediterranean trade. Second, membership in the European Union makes trade easy with the rest of Europe. And third, Greece has a huge "informal sector" that operates outside of government regulation. Small and family businesses don't register their workers, pay them off the books, and still manage to get loans and contracts. This is not the same as microfinance, where the businesses and loans are tiny. These are substantial businesses. This third reason deserves further study by the ECA: If national politics make it impractical to eliminate formal barriers to business, Greece offers an example of how an informal sector can grow beyond microfinance.

Saudi Arabia offers another kind of anomaly. It ranked

23rd in 2008. Its only low score was enforcing contracts (136th). In Saudi Arabia, contracts depend on trust rather than on legal procedure. That means it matters who you are. Men and Muslims—Arabs especially—matter most. The result is still a high score. This kind of anomaly led *Doing Business* to add a Gender Project that will "identify legal and regulatory barriers facing businesswomen in 181 countries, and to advocate change."

Despite these and other anomalies, *Doing Business* remains the best means we have to measure the health of the domestic business sector across the world. Other rankings are useful, but none has that single focus. For example, the World Economic Forum does an annual "Global Competitiveness" ranking, where the United States usually comes out on top. One key indicator is "market size," so Singapore will never rank very high. Yet in *Doing Business*, Singapore comes out on top. Most African countries can never rise very high in Global Competitiveness, but they can rise high in *Doing Business*, as Mauritius—another small country—has done so well.

The World Bank uses another set of indicators, "World Governance." Transparency International does a "Corruption Perception Index." Freedom House ranks democracy and human rights. We saw earlier that the Millennium Challenge Corporation uses a mix of seventeen indicators that include *Doing Business* but also feature democracy, human rights, public spending on health and education, and the rate of immunization. These other indicators are all excellent. Yet only *Doing Business* zeroes in on the domestic business sector. And as we saw in the case of the IBD, you can use *Doing Business* as the springboard for a sophisticated program of assistance rather than as a blunt instrument that leaves the exact same imprint on everything you hit with it.

Last but not least, let's compare *Doing Business* to the famous "Washington Consensus." In a 1990 book *Latin American Adjustment*, the British economist John Williamson summarized what he thought the World Bank and other key international economic institutions in Washington offered as useful advice for economic reform:

1. Fiscal discipline.
2. A redirection of public expenditure priorities toward fields offering both high economic returns and the potential to improve income distribution, such as primary health care, primary education, and infrastructure.
3. Tax reform (to lower marginal rates and broaden the tax base).
4. Interest rate liberalization.
5. A competitive exchange rate.
6. Trade liberalization.
7. Liberalization of inflows of foreign direct investment.
8. Privatization.
9. Deregulation (to abolish barriers to entry and exit).
10. Secure property rights.

In the years since, this "Washington consensus" has been the subject of lively debate among economists. For example, Joseph Stiglitz, who won the Nobel Prize in Economics in 2001, argued in a 2002 book, *Globalization and Its Discontents*, that the Washington consensus did more harm than good. All ten items, all at once, resulted in a cookie-cutter application that nowhere fit the specifics of a particular country. Success stories like China adopted a few items, piecemeal over the years, and in variations fitting to the time and place.

From the point of view of the domestic business sector, the ten items of the Washington consensus matter far less than the ten elements of *Doing Business*. The Consensus is mostly macroeconomic and external, about making the whole country more attractive for foreign trade and investment. *Doing Business* is microeconomic and internal, about helping each domestic business thrive. Number 9 of the Consensus, "Deregulation," is closest to *Doing Business*. Note that number 2 of the Consensus might even contradict *Doing Business*: High economic returns and better income distribution come first of all from a thriving domestic business sector. The same is true of number 8: better to let other domestic firms compete with state enterprises than to privatize what are probably bad businesses in the first place.

All in all, the sections of this chapter begin to fill out some of the myriad details for what, why, and how a new Marshall Plan for poor countries might put into practice particular elements of the original one to move them up the *Doing Business* list and help their business sectors thrive. There will be many further details to work out, other twists and turns, and many surprises along the way. But the light at the end of the tunnel is a share of the same prosperity that business has already brought to other parts of the world.

6

CONCLUSION

Make It Your Business

Every year for the past few decades, thousands of young people from rich countries enter the aid system. They come in through the existing institutions, these days often NGOs, as interns or on a short project, a study tour, or research grant. On their first trip to a poor country, many of them hit the ground and fall in love with development. It's exotic, altruistic, exciting, and it changes their whole outlook on life. They learn so much they want to keep going back. Some do. Or they might come home and go into some other career but stay involved in some way, by donating money or volunteering. Or later in life they sponsor their own project, like a well or school in a poor remote village.

This army of young and once-young people who love development are behind the recent calls in the richer countries to double or even triple aid to poor countries. Politicians, celebrities, and the aid agencies themselves play to this avid audience with great effect. Go to the Web site of Britain's *Make Poverty History* for a glimpse at the reach and ambition of what is now a global campaign. Pro-business aid can never compete in the same way. Charity touches the heart. Business does not. As we saw in the first chapter, support for the aid system has merged with religious feeling to become a modern-day crusade.

As a group, development veterans fall into step with the public campaign. As individuals, though, many fall away. You remember that the village project you loved working on did not actually work. Or it worked as long as you were there, and you know it was bound to fail soon after you left. You saw the waste of the government agencies, the SUVs of the foreign experts, and the new projects arising modeled on the old ones that did not work. You return to ordinary life in your home country and watch in silence as the pro-aid campaign bubbles around you. Or you stay in development, a good citizen in whatever agency you work for, but silently checked out, no longer believing.

The overall system will not change anytime soon, but there is much you can do while we all await the stars aligning. This chapter offers small steps you can take, because there is no General Marshall right now in the right position, with the right idea, to set things right at the vast scale we ultimately need. But in the future—who knows? A British prime minister, a U.N. secretary general, an American president or secretary of state, Bill Gates or Oprah Winfrey—

could step forward at any time to lead the way. Even that might not be enough, but in the doing is the only way to find out.

In this chapter we look at the role of private citizens, foreign companies, business associations, government aid agencies, government agencies in the poor countries, NGOs, business schools, and business students. Note who's missing: domestic companies in the poor countries. We leave them out because they're already doing what they should do: staying in business. Our aim is to urge and guide everyone else to help them succeed. As a shorthand we refer here to "companies" and "agencies," but in reality we are talking to individuals within them. Organizations don't change strategy. People do. You need individuals within a firm or agency to get the right idea to do the right thing. That's how strategy changes.

Let's start with private citizens in the poor countries themselves. If you have enough education, wealth, skill, or opportunity to make a difference at home, look first to join or assist your local business sector. Promote pro-business policies for your government. Go to your local business school. Become one of Ayittey's cheetahs. Or if your local business sector is so crippled that you find no opportunity there, work for a foreign business in your country or elsewhere if you have to. Go to a foreign business school. Do whatever you can to equip yourself to help your local business sector when the tide shifts and your country stops thwarting its business sector.

As for private citizens in rich countries, the first thing to do is make a distinction between humanitarian and economic aid when you decide how to use your charitable dollars, votes, visits, and advice. If you want to help end poverty, find a pro-business project to help. A good place to start is one of these new Web sites: businessfights poverty.org and businessactionforafrica.org. If you're interested especially in businesses that aim to help the poor in poor countries, or otherwise serve social ends that government and NGOs typically monopolize, you will discover a wealth of "social enterprise" businesses to look to instead. A good place to start your search is the online clearinghouse Nextbillion.net, a joint project of the World Resources Institute and the Acumen Fund.

Leaders and managers of foreign companies that operate in poor countries have a different puzzle to solve. You might find yourself under pressure to bribe local officials. Or you find yourself under pressure from the local government and your public at home to contribute to government or NGO projects in the country where you operate. Or the local business sector is so weak you have to take on activities like transport, banking, supply, distribution, and other services that in normal countries local businesses do. For example, you build and run your own employee housing because there is no reliable local construction or real estate business. Or you hire your own cooks because there's no reliable catering service. You buy and run trucks because there's no reliable transport company.

For the first problem: Of course you should not bribe local officials. But what if your competition does and you cannot compete if you don't do the same? There is no good answer to this. Unfortunately, the problem will persist until the local business sector grows strong enough to fight back—because bribery stunts its development even more than it hurts you.

The second and third problems are linked. Divide your budget for corporate social responsibility in two: Use half for charity in government and NGO projects, and half to help foster a local business sector. The key is to make sure that your charity money goes only for refugee, medical, or emergency relief. For economic development, support the business sector. For example, Barclays boasts that it supports 700 community groups in twenty-six countries. Why not cut that figure in half, redirect the charity side to true charity programs, and support local business with the other half. Founded in 1690, Barclays was one of the earliest firms that helped foster a healthy business sector in Britain. It can help do the same in other countries too.

Microfinance, training, and business loans are simple ways to start helping local business. The aim is to contract out to new local businesses what in normal countries you don't do yourselves. If you want to favor social enterprise even for charity, again Nextbillion is a good place to learn more.

An example of social enterprise comes from Mohammad Yunus of Grameen Bank. He begins his recent book, *Creating a World Without Poverty*, with a story of Danone, the global yogurt and water company, asking him at a lunch in Paris in 2005 what the firm could do to help in poor countries. Yunus proposed a joint nonprofit company of Grameen and Danone to produce and market their healthiest products at reduced prices in poor Bangladesh villages, and to reinvest any profits back in the company rather than pay dividends. Danone agreed. The first factory opened in 2006 in northern Bangladesh. Grameen's women borrowers peddle the yogurt from village to village. Like any business start-up, it remains to be seen whether the company succeeds over time. We do know there are immediate benefits to Bangladesh: Farmers can sell their milk locally, the factory employs local workers, and local women make money selling the yogurt. You can read about this and many other examples of social enterprise on the Nextbillion site.

Business associations have an enormous role to play in helping the business sector of poor countries. In countries with strong business sectors there are countless associations of every kind for groups of businesses in the same field. For the United States, go to the Federal Citizen Information Center Consumer Action Web site to find a list. You'll see the American Bankers Association, the American Fence Association, The Carpet and Rug Institute, and so on. They hold conferences and run Web sites to keep their members educated on the latest innovations in their fields, and they lobby government agencies for rules that help their members. There are location-based associations that bring together different kinds of businesses too, like the

Rotary Club, Kiwanis, and Chambers of Commerce. Many of these associations have international versions, but very few operate in poor countries. Of course they can't lobby in other nations, but they can run conferences and Web sites to help foster and strengthen local business associations. This is also a way for foreign companies to help in the poor countries where they operate: Fund activities of your business association there.

Next, what can government aid agencies do? These include the bilaterals, like USAID, the Agence Française de Développement, Japan's International Cooperation Agency, the Danish International Development Agency, and so on. Then there are the multilaterals, like the World Bank and the United Nations Development Programme. Overall, the bi- and multilaterals are an obstacle. They spend most of the world's aid, and they overwhelmingly spend it on government projects in poor countries. Most have small programs to support local business in some way. All we can say is they should do more of that and less of other kinds of economic development. And as they do that, they must beware of the "allanblackia problem," where their project staff do too many tasks that local businesses should do instead. If you work for one of these agencies and it refuses to change, try to transfer to whatever small pro-business projects it does do and continue to advocate and wait for more.

Government agencies in the poor countries remain a big problem, as wards in part of the current system. There is little short-term incentive for them to change. Like the foreign agencies, most have some small pro-business projects, usually funded from outside. Again, they should do more of those and less of their traditional government development projects. The same is true for lone individuals in agencies that refuse to change: Try to transfer to some pro-business project and speak up when you are able about helping local business more. For example, circulate the *Doing Business* report and discuss it internally. Some agencies might consider that subversive activity, so understand the risks before you decide to act.

Foreign NGOs can also be a problem. If an NGO distributes free yogurt and bottled water to poor Bangladeshi villages, how can Grameen's joint venture with Danone even get off the ground? Foreign NGOs especially crowd out smaller or family businesses with very small profit margins and niches among the poor themselves. They began and continue to excel in refugee, medical, or emergency relief, which by nature calls for charity rather than business. But most have grown even bigger development arms where they run long-term projects in nonrefugee villages that make it next to impossible for local businesses to compete there. So foreign NGOs should go back to pure charity for refugees and emergency relief, and get out of economic development completely. Or, they can convert to social enterprise instead.

Local NGOs are mostly mirror images of foreign NGOs, which fund them. So they too should stick to charity for refugee, medical, and emergency relief and get out of economic development, or also convert to social enterprise. Or maybe their current staff are the future staff of fully pro-business NGOs like local business associations. Once a nation achieves a somewhat normal business sector, a normal local philanthropy sector can grow up alongside it. We especially see that in India today: The Concern India Foundation and the Charities Aid Foundation India are just two examples among many of modern charities founded in the past two decades from India's new business prosperity.

Last but not least, we see a special role for business schools and their students in poor countries of the world. In 1959 the Carnegie and Ford foundations issued reports that advocated across the United States an upgrade from low-level business colleges to the professional business schools we know today. The phenomenon spread widely to other strong business sectors, especially Europe. In the past two decades, the number of business schools in China has grown from zero to more than 100, and the number continues to grow fast. India now has more than 1,000. All poor countries need business schools. To get started, foreign business schools can help.

Above all, poor countries need normal business schools that support their local business sectors with dedicated research and trained graduates. A local alumni network becomes yet another pro-business association. And the local business school can offer research and seminars that help a country move up the *Doing Business* list. Today most business schools in poor countries are even behind the low-level schools that Carnegie and Ford found in the United States half a century ago. Or the business school is a state agency that trains managers from other state agencies rather than for business.

Aid projects over the past forty years boasted countless partnership projects where a bilateral agency of a rich country funded its own universities to help upgrade local universities in poor countries. Almost always they left out the business school. Every major business school in a poor country needs a full-scale partnership project with at least one major business school in a rich country. There's a worthy cause for bilateral agencies to fund. But beware: The past partnership projects overwhelmingly helped the rich university far more than the poor one. Most of the money went to help make faculty from the rich country experts in the poor country. Many local faculty did well as individuals: They got master's and doctorate degrees at the rich university and came back to promotions or stayed in the rich country as professors. But overall the local university came out last.

So a business school partnership program must avoid such mistakes and instead aim to do what major business schools do so well: Plug into their surrounding business sector. That is, they should help above all to promote a strong relationship between the local business school and the local business sector, rather than just a bilateral relationship between the rich and poor business schools. So alumni networks and *Doing Business* projects must be part of the partnership from the start. And the local business school should become just as key to local social enterprise.

Business school students can help. In rich countries, social enterprise is booming among most major business schools. It's common to find that a quarter of all business students are members of the school's social enterprise club. They have their own international club, Net Impact, with hundreds of chapters. You find them on every continent and in a growing list of poorer countries, not only Brazil and India but also Bangladesh, Ghana, and Peru. The school's own social enterprise program and Net Impact sponsor all kinds of field projects where business students travel to work for social enterprises in poor countries. That alone is worthwhile, and it is not much of a stretch to expand that to include regular small businesses in poor countries too. These kinds of projects are natural targets for multinational companies that send their staff to volunteer for a time in poor countries, because business schools already have connections or even alumni at these companies.

Thanks in part to the social enterprise movement, the MBA degree in rich countries is becoming the leading general graduate degree in all fields of work. This reflects above all that business is the main employer in rich countries, and a graduate degree gets you a better job in that sector. And business skills and method can help other fields run better too. If pro-business aid ever takes off, these MBA graduates can be its future foot soldiers, in the same way an earlier generation went overseas on government and NGO projects to help save the world.

In the poor countries themselves, local business school graduates are the future foot soldiers of their own thriving business sectors. How long that will take depends on the country. And there is no guarantee, anywhere, that it will happen at all. As in countries that are already rich, a thriving local business sector in every poor country will be the fruit of a long, hard struggle. Aid can help, in the form of our new Marshall Plan. In the meantime, aid must at least do no harm, and right now that's what it's doing.

Business must come first in solving the problem of poverty, but there are many problems it can't solve. It certainly has its limits. There will always be a need for charities of various kinds, to help the ill and destitute, for medical research, and for countless other worthy causes. There will always be a need for government agencies to provide public services like police and roads. Business makes the prosperity that pays for those activities, but it cannot and should not run them itself, because it can't make a profit. Social enterprise can take some of the burden, because it often tries just to break even or operates with some kind of subsidy. And the precise balance among the three sectors—business, NGO, government—changes through time and often turns into rivalry. For example, you find hospitals of all three kinds, and fierce debates about which kind is best. We can at least say here that not all hospitals, always, should run as pure businesses.

By all means, business cannot solve all the world's problems. It is hardly a charitable enterprise, and certainly has its share of crooks. Governments and NGOs do too. You need a strong legal system to catch them all. Elaborate auditing and reporting laws in prosperous countries aim to catch corporate thieves. Parallel rules target governments and NGOs. Transparency International monitors corruption in all three sectors. A strong business sector means the country has the incentive and funding to fight corruption. An individual business might benefit from bribing a government official, but if that firm has lots of competitors they will cry foul. The business sector as a whole doesn't like bribes. They're an extra government tax. Yet business will never be completely free of bribery and theft. You have to police it forever.

Another negative side of business is its natural role to make winners and losers in the short run, which can last a very long time. Carthage imitated Roman pottery and put the original Italians out of business for centuries. The rise and fall of particular fortunes make for a very old story. That will never change.

We could list other flaws, but the point is clear enough: Business is a very imperfect system to say the least. But remember what Winston Churchill said about politics, some time after Britain voted him out of power despite his leadership through World War II: "Democracy is the worst form of government, except for all those other forms that have been tried from time to time." In the same way we can look at competing economic systems through history: tribal, despotic, feudal, pure and national socialism, and the aidism of government and NGO projects. We can only conclude, in the spirit of Churchill: Business is the worst path to prosperity, except for all the others.

A NOTE ON RELATED RESEARCH

We wrote this book as an extended essay on the power of business to transform the economies of the poorest nations as it has transformed those of the now-industrial world, or those making the transition from socialism to private enterprise. Our focus was on business rather than on the broader philosophical questions about capitalism, to emphasize the uncoordinated, micro elements of economic transformation. We use the Marshall Plan as the example of a policy initiative to let loose individual market forces, as opposed to planning initiatives. We linked these themes of business as a change agent and policy force that can shape that potential on four previous occasions: Our opinion-piece in the *Financial Times* on June 4, 2007, on the sixtieth anniversary of George Marshall's celebrated commencement address at Harvard University; Duggan's Columbia Business School working paper of 2006, "A Marshall Plan for Africa?"; and Hubbard's University lecture at Columbia in May 2006 and Cairncross lecture at Oxford University in June 2007.

There is a rich body of scholarly research on problems and opportunities in economic development in Africa since 1960, which we consulted and list in our bibliography. Our essay does not attempt to comment directly on or do justice to that work. Our discussion does, though, fit squarely within the tension in approaches to Western aid to Africa between "transformations" and more "marginal steps," as in William Easterly's essay "Can the West Save Africa?" We clearly fall into the second category.

This tension in economic research and practice is as old as the postcolonial period in Africa itself. Gordon Brown's big push to end African poverty, which we discussed in our essay, or Jeffrey Sachs's call for a financial big push in his popular treatise *The End of Poverty* call to mind the "Big Push" suggested in the earlier economic writings of Paul Rosenstein-Rodan and Walt Rostow, who argued that coordinated, macro changes were required to produce "balanced growth." Reflecting a more Hayekian spirit of uncoordinated elements of growth, Albert Hirschman emphasized "unbalanced growth," and P. T. Bauer sharply critiqued the Big Push. This debate, well chronicled in Easterly's essay, continued into the 1990s, as researchers debated whether "shock therapy" or "gradualism" was the better policy course for economies in transition from Communist central planning to more decentralized market mechanisms.

And, in the past decade, the Big Push idea has returned again to Africa. In *The End of Poverty* Sachs makes a compelling *moral* argument for the West to save Africa. But, as a matter of economics, *how*? Sachs argues for a U.S. aid budget of 0.7 percent of GDP, substantially higher than the present level. How such largesse is to lead to transformation and growth is not clear, however. As a matter of fact, the West spent $714 billion in current dollars on aid to Africa between 1960 and 2006. It is also by no means clear whether "aid" is the answer if "growth" is the question, as Craig Burnside and David Dollar; William Easterly, Ross Levine, and David Roodman; and Raghuram Rajan and Arvind Subramanian have persuasively argued.

While Sachs evokes the imagery of the Marshall Plan for Europe, he seems to think of the Marshall Plan as a top-down Big Push mechanism. As we argue here, we do not accept this reading of the intent or execution of the Marshall Plan. Indeed, it is precisely the micro, business-promoting features of the Marshall Plan for Europe that led us to recommend its application to the thornier problem of stimulating African economic growth.

Paul Collier, a distinguished Oxford scholar of African development, writes eloquently in *The Bottom Billion* that African societies coexist with the twenty-first century but that their reality lies in the fourteenth century: "civil war, plague, ignorance." As Easterly notes in his essay, though, although African countries score poorly on measures of bad government and civil war, which Collier and others

169

stress, their relative overrepresentation in these is less than that for income, poverty, and social indicators emphasized by economists and aid officials.

In his wonderful text of economic analysis and compelling stories, William Easterly's *The White Man's Burden* assumes the anti–Big Push mantle in evaluating aid and the contemporary African experience. Easterly is critical of aid institutions and the lack of emphasis on business on the practice of aid. And he rightly points out that Big Push ideas are periodically recycled—from Lord Hailey's 1938 survey for the Committee on African Research for the British government to the Millennium Development Goals and exhortations from Jeffrey Sachs or Bono almost seventy years later—with little evidence of success in between.

Although we very much agree with Easterly in spirit, we can also agree somewhat with Collier that, "Aid is part of the solution, not part of the problem." More precisely: "Aid *can be, should be* part of the solution, not *just* part of the problem." But the question is *how*?

There is, for example, a lack of consensus among leading economists in a list of Big Push policy actions, the application of which would raise growth. Easterly cites a statement by leading academic economists in a 2004 conference, called the Barcelona Development Agenda, that "there is no single set of policies that can be guaranteed to ignite sustained growth." The May 2008 report of the World Bank–sponsored Growth Commission accepted this statement. By contrast, much more consensus among economists exists for the power of a vibrant business sector in making possible entrepreneurship, innovation, and growth. Easterly's essay notes, for example, that the largest sustained per capita growth outliers in recent years are the East Asian tigers, India, China, and Africa's Botswana and Mauritius, all thanks to business, not aid.

Again, our reading of economic research and development practice does not lead us to share the polar view that aid programs are necessarily unproductive or harmful. Even Easterly ends his book with ways to improve aid, rather than just eliminate it. Indeed, we admire in broad brush the U.S. Millennium Challenge Account initiative, which Hubbard helped design, for its attempt to condition additional aid on institutional reforms that could promote business development. Upon closer inspection, though, the Millennium Challenge Account reverts to a top-down approach—again, more of an explicit attempt at "transformation," to use Easterly's term, than we recommend here.

But a Marshall Plan for Africa and other poor countries would be an important positive step in reforming Western aid and increasing the likelihood of its success in advancing economic growth. Yes, attaining this goal requires financial commitments, but it also demands the decentralized structure, business-promoting features, and key roles for business leaders that characterized the Marshall Plan for Europe.

We are aware that all interventions, including the one we propose here, must confront the basic political economy question of why economics might be pursuing antigrowth policies in the first place. Raghuram Rajan and Luigi Zingales have described, for example, a development trap as an initial allocation of endowments such that constituencies created by those endowments successfully support bad policies that reproduce those initial constituencies over time. In Africa, they argue, a relatively small, educated urban middle class has often sided with a small ruling elite in opposing wide and deep market reforms. They argue that sequencing of reforms is likely important. Our Marshall Plan approach would do exactly this. Education and business skill development can be externally supported. Then external support can encourage reforms that produce growth. Economic growth can create greater opportunities, which in turn reduce the incentives of the privileged to defend their rents, and instead cause them to focus on reforms that remove impediments to taking advantage of opportunities.

Our overriding point remains an agreement with George Marshall's very clear observation that the "breakdown of the business structure of Europe during the war" was the problem that aid must solve. That solution is much more about normalcy than it is about grand transformation, as Marshall himself clearly realized.

ECA	YEARS			
	1	**2**	**3**	**4**
A New Funding ($M)	10,000	10,000	10,000	10,000
B From Previous Year ($M)	0	8,016	14,054	18,110
C Total Funds ($M)	10,000	18,016	24,054	28,110
D Participating Countries: New	10	10	10	10
E Participating Countries: Total	10	20	30	40
F Loans per Country ($M)	165	165	165	165
G Loans Made ($M)	1,653	3,302	4,953	6,600
H Administration @ 20% ($M)	331	660	991	1,320
I Loans Unpaid @ 20% ($M)	331	660	991	1,320
J Loans Repaid @ 80% ($M)	1,322	2,642	3,962	5,280
K Interest @ 20% ($M)	264	528	792	1,056
L Net Funds ($M)	9,603	17,224	22,865	26,526
M Country Development ($M)	1,587	3,170	4,755	6,336
N To Next Year ($M)	8,016	14,054	18,110	20,190

A MARSHALL PLAN BUDGET

This budget gives a general picture of how a Marshall Plan for poor countries might receive and spend money over ten years. It gives only an illustration: ECA staff would work out the budget with funders and participating countries, as in the original.

5	6	7	8	9	10	TOTAL
10,000	10,000	10,000	10,000	10,000	10,000	100,000
20,190	20,290	18,410	14,550	9,700	4,850	
30,190	30,290	28,410	24,550	19,700	14,850	
10	10	10	5	0	0	75
50	60	70	75	75	75	75
165	165	165	165	165	165	
8,250	9,900	11,550	12,375	12,375	12,375	83,333
1,650	1,980	2,310	2,475	2,475	2,475	16,667
1,650	1,980	2,310	2,475	2,475	2,475	16,667
6,600	7,920	9,240	9,900	9,900	9,900	66,666
1,320	1,584	1,848	1,980	1,980	1,980	13,333
28,210	27,914	25,638	21,580	16,730	11,880	
7,920	9,504	11,088	11,880	11,880	11,880	80,000
20,290	18,410	14,550	9,700	4,850	0	

ECA	YEARS			
	1	**2**	**3**	**4**
O New Funding ($M)	1,000	1,000	1,000	1,000
P Net Funds Available ($M)	1,000	2,000	3,000	4,000
Q Capital Growth @ 5% ($M)	50	100	150	200
R Total Spending @ 5% ($M)	50	100	150	200
S Administration @ 20% ($M)	10	20	30	40
T Grant Funds @ 80% (M)	40	80	120	160

BUDGET NOTES

A   Total world aid per year ($100B) × 10%.

B   Carry-over from row N of the previous year.

C   A + B.

D   The lower half of the *Doing Business* rankings gives us about seventy-five target countries. We phase them in over the first eight years, so that all countries get at least three years of support.

E   D plus row E of the previous year.

F   We use a figure that works out to zero funds left over in year 10, row N, rounding to millions as needed.

G   E × F. Decimals rounded in row F show up in this row.

H   G × 20%. This is a high administrative cost for a loan program, but providing essential due diligence and financial controls merit the expense. The program will quickly become one of the leading employers of accountants from poor countries, who might need extra training tailored to the program.

I   G × 20%. This is likely too high a number, but it is better to overestimate the problems ahead than to underestimate them.

5	6	7	8	9	10	TOTAL
1,000	1,000	1,000	1,000	1,000	1,000	**10,000**
5,000	6,000	7,000	8,000	9,000	10,000	
250	300	350	400	450	500	**2,750**
250	300	350	400	450	500	**2,750**
50	60	70	80	90	100	**550**
200	240	280	320	360	400	**2,200**

BUDGET NOTES *(CONTINUED)*

J   G × 80%. This is likely too low a number. See I above.

K   J × 20%. The actual interest rate will vary by country and type of loan, most likely from 0 to 30%.

L   A – G – H + J + K.

M   J + K. These are the funds available to the local country for economic infrastructure projects.

N   L – M. There will be investment income from funds not loaned out that year, so this is likely an underestimate.

O   Total world aid per year ($100B) × 1%.

P   O plus carry-over from row P of the previous year. Year 10's amount goes to fund Year 11 of the ECA loan program.

Q   P × 5%. This is likely a conservative estimate of annual investment income.

R   P × 5%. These are funds available to spend. See Q above.

S   R × 20%. This is typical for grant-making foundations.

T   R × 80%. See S above. These are the funds available to spend on grants every year.

BIBLIOGRAPHY

Each of the several topics this book touches on has a rich and varied literature. Here we list only books and a few key articles and reports, including any work cited in the text.

Achebe, Chinua. *No Longer at Ease*. New York: Obolensky, 1961.
———. *A Man of the People*. Garden City, N.Y.: Doubleday, 1967.
Aghion, Beatriz de, and Jonathan Morduch. *The Economics of Microfinance*. Cambridge, Mass.: MIT Press, 2005.
Alexander, Sidney. "The Marshall Plan," Planning pamphlets 60–61, National Planning Association, Washington, D.C., 1948.
Amatori, Franco, and Geoffrey Jones. *Business History Around the World*. Cambridge: Cambridge University Press, 2003.
Artadi, Elsa, and Xavier Sala-i-Martin. "The Economic Tragedy of the XXth Century: Growth in Africa," National Bureau of Economic Research, Working Paper 9865, July 2003.
Aubert, Jean-Jacques. *Business Managers in Ancient Rome*. Leiden: E. J. Brill, 1994.
Ayittey, George. *Africa Unchained*. New York: Palgrave Macmillan, 2005.
Bates, Robert. *Markets and States in Tropical Africa*. Berkeley: University of California Press, 1981.

Baumol, William. *The Free-Market Innovation Machine.* Princeton: Princeton University Press, 2002.

———, Robert Litan, and Carl Schramm. *Good Capitalism, Bad Capitalism.* New Haven: Yale University Press, 2007.

Beard, Charles. *An Economic Interpretation of the Constitution of the United States.* New York: Macmillan, 1914.

Berg, Elliott. *Accelerated Development in Sub-Saharan Africa.* Washington, D.C.: World Bank, 1981.

Bhidé, Amar. *The Origin and Evolution of New Businesses.* New York: Oxford University Press, 2000.

———. *The Venturesome Economy.* Princeton: Princeton University Press, 2008.

Bishop, Matthew, and Michael Green. *Philanthrocapitalism.* London: Bloomsbury Press, 2008.

Bloch, Marc. *French Rural History.* London: Routledge & Kegan Paul, 1966.

Bornstein, David. *How to Change the World.* New York: Oxford University Press, 2004.

Brainerd, Lael, et al. *The Other War.* Washington, D.C.: Brookings Institution Press, 2003.

Braudel, Fernand. *Capitalism and Material Life, 1400–1800.* New York: Harper & Row, 1973.

Burnside, Craig, and David Dollar. "Aid, Policies, and Growth," *American Economic Review*, 90 (September 2000).

Cameron, Rondo, and Larry Neal. *A Concise Economic History of the World*, 4th edition. New York: Oxford University Press, 2003.

Chen, Shaohua, and Martin Ravallion. "The developing world is poorer than we thought, but no less successful in the fight against poverty," World Bank Policy Research working paper, WPS 4703 (August 1, 2008).

Chenery, Hollis. "Approaches to Development Planning," Discussion Paper. No. 5. Washington, D.C.: U.S. Agency for Inter-national Development, 1962.

———, and Alan Strout. "Foreign Assistance and Economic Development," *American Economic Review* 56(4), part 1 (September 1966).

Cheru, Fantu, and Colin Bradford. *The Millennium Development Goals.* Helsinki: Zed Books, 2005.

Clark, Heather. *When There Was No Money.* New York: Springer, 2006.

Collier, Paul. *The Bottom Billion.* New York: Oxford University Press, 2007.

Commission on Growth and Development, *The Growth Report: Strategies for Sustained Growth and Inclusive Development.* Washington, D.C.: World Bank, 2008.

Diamond, Jared. *Guns, Germs and Steel.* New York: Norton, 1997.

Easterly, William. *The Elusive Quest for Growth.* Cambridge, Mass.: MIT Press, 2001.

———. *The White Man's Burden.* New York: Penguin Press, 2006.

———. "Can the West Save Africa?" working paper no. 14363, National Bureau of Economic Research (September 2008).

———, editor. *Reinventing Foreign Aid.* Cambridge, Mass.: MIT Press, 2008.

———, Ross Levine, and David Roodman. "New Data, New Doubts: A Comment on Burnside and Dollar's 'Aid, Policies, and Growth'," *American Economic Review*, 94 (June 2004).

Ellsworth, Lynn. "Good Practice in Competitive Grant-Making," APAP research report no. 1037, Sustainable Financing Initiative. Washington, D.C.: Abt Associates, 1998.

———. "The Road to Financial Sustainability," USAID, SD Publications Series, technical paper no. 85. Washington, D.C., January 1998.

Faure, David. *China and Capitalism.* Hong Kong: Hong Kong University Press, 2006.

Ferguson, Niall. *The Ascent of Money.* New York: Penguin Press, 2008.

Fisman, Ray. *Economic Gangsters.* Princeton: Princeton University Press, 2008.

Forum Barcelona 2004, "The Barcelona Development Agenda."

Francks, Penelope. *Agriculture and Economic Development in East Asia.* London: Routledge, 1999.

———. *Rural Economic Development in Japan.* London: Routledge, 2006.

Ghana, Commission of Enquiry into Irregularities and Malpractices in the Grant of Import Licenses. "Summary of the Report." Accra-Tema: Ministry of Information, 1967.

Goetzman, William, and K. Geert Rouwenhorst. *The Origins of Value.* New York: Oxford University Press, 2005.

Gordon, Robert, and James Howell. *Higher Education for Business.* New York: Columbia University Press, 1959.

Hailey, William. *An African Survey.* London: Oxford University Press, 1938.

———. *African Survey.* London: Oxford University Press, 1957.

———. *African Economic Development.* New York: Harper & Brothers, 1958.

———. *The Geography of Modern Africa.* New York: Columbia University Press, 1964.

Heck, Gene. *Charlemagne, Muhammad, and the Arab Roots of Capitalism.* Berlin: Walter de Gruyter, 2006.

Herold, J. C. *The Age of Napoleon*. New York: American Heritage, 1963.

Hirschman, Albert. *The Strategy of Economic Development*. New Haven: Yale University Press, 1958.

———. *Development Projects Observed*. Washington, D.C.: Brookings Institution, 1967.

Hoffman, Stanley, and Charles Maier, editors. *Marshall Plan: A Retrospective*. Boulder, Colo.: Westview Press, 1984.

Hunt, Edwin, and James Murray. *A History of Business in Medieval Europe*. Cambridge: Cambridge University Press, 1999.

Jones, Geoffrey, and Jonathan Zeitlin. *The Oxford Handbook of Business History*. Oxford: Oxford University Press, 2008.

Kennedy, Paul. *African Capitalism*. Cambridge: Cambridge University Press, 1988.

Killick, Tony. *Development Economics in Action*. New York: St. Martin's, 1978.

Kinsley, Michael. *Creative Capitalism*. New York: Simon & Schuster, 2008.

Landes, David. *The Wealth and Poverty of Nations*. New York: Norton, 1998.

Lele, Uma. *The Design of Rural Development*. Baltimore: Johns Hopkins University Press, 1975.

Leontief, Wassily. *Input-Output Economics*. New York: Oxford University Press, 1966.

Lewis, W. A. *The Theory of Economic Growth*. London: Allen & Unwin, 1955.

Lipton, Michael. *Why Poor People Stay Poor*. London: Temple Smith, 1976.

Lodge, George, and Craig Wilson. *A Corporate Solution to Global Poverty*. Princeton: Princeton University Press, 2006.

Lopez, Robert. *The Commercial Revolution of the Middle Ages*. Englewood Cliffs, N.J.: Prentice-Hall, 1971.

Lübeck, Paul. *The African Bourgeoisie*. Boulder, Colo.: Lynne Rienner, 1987.

Maddison, Angus. *Chinese Economic Performance in the Long Run*. Paris: Organisation for Economic Co-operation and Development, 1998.

———. *The World Economy: Historical Statistics*. Paris: Organisation for Economic Co-operation and Development, 2003.

McCloskey, Deirdre. *The Vices of Economists, the Virtues of the Bourgeoisie*. Amsterdam: Amsterdam University Press, 1996.

Mee, Charles. *The Marshall Plan*. New York: Simon & Schuster, 1984.

Mellor, John. *Economics of Agricultural Development*. Ithaca: Cornell University Press, 1966.

———, editor. *Agriculture on the Road to Industrialization*. Baltimore: Johns Hopkins University Press, 1995.

Menges, Constantine, editor. *The Marshall Plan from Those Who Made It Succeed*. Lanham, Md.: University Press of America, 1999.

Mishkin, Frederic. *The Next Great Globalization*. Princeton: Princeton University Press, 2006.

Moore, Barrington. *Social Origins of Dictatorship and Democracy*. Boston: Beacon Press, 1967.

Mosher, Arthur. *Getting Agriculture Moving*. New York: Praeger, 1966.

Moyo, Dambisa. *Dead Aid*. New York: Penguin, 2009.

Needham, Joseph. *Science and Civilisation in China*. Cambridge: Cambridge University Press, 1954.

Pierson, Frank, et al. *The Education of American Businessmen*. New York: McGraw-Hill, 1959.

Polak, Paul. *Out of Poverty*. San Francisco: Berrett-Koehler, 2008.

Polanyi, Karl. *The Great Transformation*. New York: Farrar & Rinehart, 1944.

———, et al., editors. *Trade and Market in the Early Empires*. Glencoe, Ill.: Free Press, 1957.

Porter, Michael, Klaus Schwab, and Xavier Sala-i-Martin. *The Global Competitiveness Report*. Geneva: World Economic Forum, 2007.

Powelson, John. *Centuries of Economic Endeavor*. Ann Arbor: University of Michigan Press, 1994.

Prahalad, C. K. *The Fortune at the Bottom of the Pyramid*. Upper Saddle River, N.J.: Wharton School Publishing, 2005.

Price, Harry. *The Marshall Plan and Its Meaning*. Ithaca: Cornell University Press.

Rajan, Raghuram, and Arvind Subramanian. "Aid and Growth: What Does the Cross-Country Evidence Show?" *Review of Economics and Statistics*, 90 (2008).

———, and Luigi Zingales. "The Persistence of Underdevelopment: Institutions, Human Capital, or Constituencies?" Working paper no. 12093, National Bureau of Economic Research (March 2006).

Rangan, V. Kasturi, et al. *Business Solutions for the Global Poor*. San Francisco: Jossey-Bass, 2007.

Riddell, Roger. *Does Foreign Aid Really Work?* New York: Oxford University Press, 2008.

Rodrik, Dani. *One Economics, Many Recipes*. Princeton: Princeton University Press, 2007.

Rosenstein-Rodan, Paul. "Problems of Industrialization of Eastern and South-eastern Europe." *Economic Journal*, 53 (1943).

Rostow, W. W. *The Stages of Economic Growth*. Cambridge: Cambridge University Press, 1960.

Sachs, Jeffrey. *The End of Poverty*. New York: Penguin Press, 2005.

———. *Common Wealth*. New York: Penguin Press, 2008.

Schain, Martin, editor. *The Marshall Plan: Fifty Years After*. New York: Palgrave, 2001.

Schama, Simon. *The Embarrassment of Riches*. New York: Knopf, 1987.

Schumpeter, Joseph. *Essays*. Cambridge, Mass.: Addison-Wesley Press, 1951.

Sender, John, and Sheila Smith. *The Development of Capitalism in Africa*. London: Metheun, 1986.

Shell Foundation, *Enterprise Solutions to Poverty* (www.shell foundation.org).

Singer, Peter. *The Life You Can Save*. New York: Random House, 2009.

Smith, Adam. *Inquiry into the Nature and Causes of the Wealth of Nations*. London: Strahan and Cadell, 1776.

Smith, Stephen. *Ending Global Poverty*. New York: Palgrave Macmillan, 2005.

Solow, R. M. *Capital Theory*. New York: Oxford University Press, 1970.

Soto, Hernando de. *The Other Path*. New York: HarperCollins, 1989.

———. *The Mystery of Capital*. New York: Basic Books, 2000.

Stiglitz, Joseph. *Globalization and Its Discontents*. New York: Norton, 2002.

Tangri, Robert. *The Politics of Patronage in Africa*. Trenton, N.J.: Africa World Press, 1999.

Tax, Sol. *Penny Capitalism*. Washington, D.C.: Smithsonian Institution, 1953.

United Kingdom, Department for International Development. *Private Sector Development Strategy*. London, 2008.

United Nations. *Delivering on the Global Partnership for Achieving the Millennium Development Goals*, MDG Gap Task Force Report. New York: United Nations, 2008.

United Nations Millennium Project. *Investing in Development.* New York: United Nations, 2005.

United States Economic Cooperation Administration. "Information for American Businessmen on the Marshall Plan." Washington, D.C.: U.S. Government Printing Office, 1949.

United States Mutual Security Agency, Mission to Greece. "The Story of the American Marshall Plan in Greece," Press Release No. 1300 (n.p, n.d.).

Wallach, Bret. *Losing Asia.* Baltimore: Johns Hopkins University Press, 1996.

Whitaker, Jennifer. *How Can Africa Survive?* New York: Council on Foreign Relations Press, 1988.

Williamson, John, editor. *Latin American Adjustment.* Washington, D.C.: Institute for International Economics, 1990.

Wilson, Craig, and Peter Wilson. *Make Poverty Business.* Sheffield: Greenleaf, 2006.

World Bank. *Doing Business.* Washington, D.C.: World Bank, 2004–2008.

Yunus, Muhammad. *Banker to the Poor.* New York: Public Affairs, 1999.

———. *Creating a World Without Poverty.* New York: Public Affairs, 2007.

INDEX